THEN & NOW

ARMORY SQUARE

Opposite: Loew's State Theater in 1954 was showing *Last Time I Saw Paris* with Elizabeth Taylor. Fifty-four years later, in October 2008, at this same theater was the world premiere of *The Express*, the story of Ernie Davis, the All-America running back from Syracuse University and the first African American to win the Heisman Trophy. (Courtesy of the Onondaga Historical Association.)

THEN & NOW

ARMORY SQUARE

Robert J. Podfigurny and George W. Curry
for the Armory Square Association

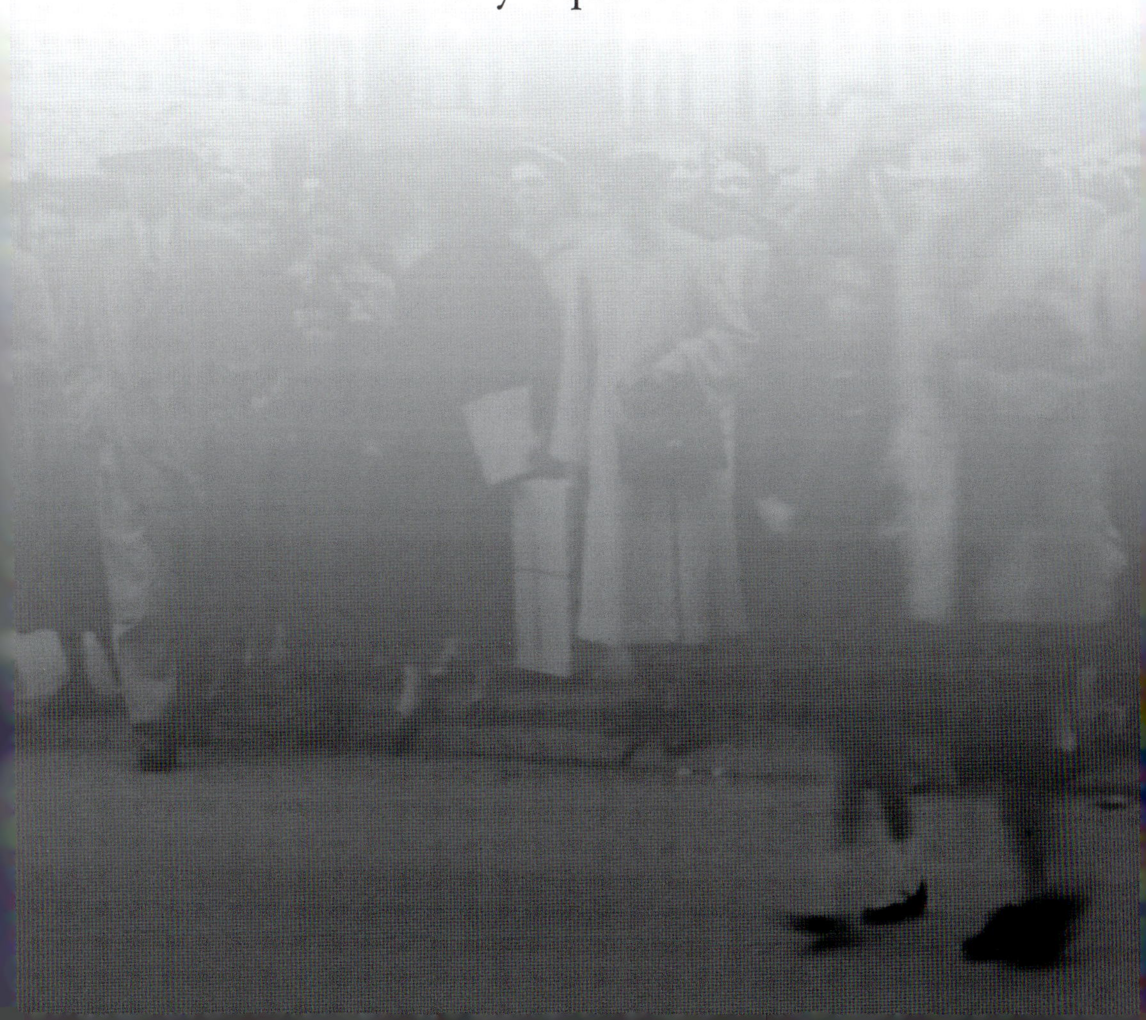

This book is dedicated to all the historic preservationists, entrepreneurs, and pioneers whose combined hard work, risks, and continued efforts have made Armory Square what it is today. And to the men and women who volunteer their time on behalf of the Armory Square Association.

ISBN 978-0-7385-6508-8

Library of Congress Control Number: 2008942671

Published by Arcadia Publishing
Charleston, South Carolina

Printed in the United States of America

For all general information contact Arcadia Publishing at:
Telephone 843-853-2070
Fax 843-853-0044
E-mail sales@arcadiapublishing.com

Visit us on the Internet at www.arcadiapublishing.com

On the front cover: Please see page 49. (Courtesy of the Onondaga Historical Association.)

On the back cover: This early-1900s photograph is of the 1874 Jefferson Street Armory designed by noted Syracuse architect Horatio Nelson White. The first armory built prior to this in 1859 was destroyed by a fire in 1872. (Courtesy of the Onondaga Historical Association.)

Contents

Acknowledgments

We would like to thank several people and organizations for their aid and assistance in bringing this book to fruition. The Onondaga Historical Association's wonderful collection was the source of many historic photographs and provided a wealth of information. Thank you to Gregg Tripoli, executive director; Dennis Connors, curator of history; Michael Flanagan, archivist and research associate; and Karen Cooney, support services administrator, without all of whom this book could not have been produced.

We would also like to thank the researchers and authors of two documents: Evamaria Hardin's 1993 book *Syracuse Landmarks—An AIA Guide to Downtown and Historic Neighborhoods* and Cynthia Carters's 2008 National Register of Historic Places registration form "South Salina Street Downtown Historic District." Both of these were invaluable to this project.

Special thanks to Kristin M. Leeder, an Upstate New York–area photographer, for her work in assisting with much of the contemporary photography. Thank you also to our editor, Rebekah Collinsworth, for her help along the way.

Last but not least, a very sincere thank-you for the generous support for this project from the following: the Downtown Committee of Syracuse; Joe Rainone of Mulrooney's Pub; Rich Sykes and RHS Holdings, LLC; Rick Tait and Pioneer Companies; and the Armory Square Association.

Unless otherwise noted, all historic images are from the collection of the Onondaga Historical Association and all contemporary images are by Kristin M. Leeder and Robert J. Podfigurny.

Introduction

The early history of the Armory Square district of downtown Syracuse is similar to the stories of countless cities and towns across the United States. The district—like the city of Syracuse itself—was settled and continued to develop through the years because of its fortunate geography and the natural resources. But as years went by and industries became less dependent on these factors, the development and overall state of this historic neighborhood would begin to decline.

In time, like many great, inspirational stories, Armory Square staged a comeback from a state of despair to begin a triumphant return. Although the district would rise and fall with the prosperity of the railroad industry, today this urban neighborhood continues to grow with continued development in a new economy. While businesses that make up modern Armory Square may be vastly different from those that first appeared over a century and a half ago, thanks to the efforts of historic preservationists and entrepreneurs alike, many of the structures remain intact—along with the strong character of this neighborhood.

In 1804, the State of New York sold an area of land that included what is now known as Armory Square to Abraham Walton of Albany for $6,550 (just $26 per acre at the time). The funds were needed for development of roadways that were integral to the transportation of salt—a plentiful resource in Syracuse, or as it is known, "the Salt City." This section became known then as the Walton Tract. Walton—the namesake for Walton Street in Armory Square—wanted to make use of the creek on the western side of the Walton Tract, so he constructed a millpond on his new plot of land. A dam in Onondaga Creek provided power for the early grain and lumber industries. A large portion of the area remained a millpond for decades until, with the advent of steam engines, the need to be near water for power became less necessary for industries.

In 1848, it was decided by the state legislature that in order to rid the area of mosquitoes that had brought about frequent epidemics of malaria, the pond was to be filled in. Soon after, streets were constructed in the area along with the oval-shaped Jefferson Park. In 1859, Jefferson Park became the site of the first armory, which was designed by local architect Horatio Nelson White. The Jefferson Street Armory provided housing for troops that fought in the Civil War. After a fire destroyed the first, a second armory (also designed by White) was constructed in 1874, and through the years to follow, it would serve as a drill center as well as provide military office space and a depository for equipment and arms. The building today is actually three separate buildings as it was expanded to accommodate changing needs.

The 1820s would bring the Erie Canal through downtown Syracuse, and in the 1830s, the railroad industry came through Syracuse on Washington Street. Two railroad companies, the Delaware, Lackawanna and Western Railroad (north-to-south train) and the New York Central Railroad (east-to-west train), both built stations in Armory Square. With these developments came a great deal of business activity in the area. The many railroad employees and passengers passing through the neighborhood spawned a boom in hotel building, as well as the addition of shops and factories for a variety of industries. A significant portion of the historic buildings in the area were constructed during this boom in the mid-19th century.

But just as the millpond was filled in, the same fate would befall the Erie Canal in 1923. The railroad tracks of the New York Central Railroad too were removed from downtown Syracuse in 1936 and relocated north to an elevated track north of Erie Boulevard. A major blow to the area businesses, many began to close up shop or relocate. In the mid-1900s, many buildings were left vacant, some were eventually razed, and parking lots began to spring up in their stead as automobiles became more prevalent. Armory Square became a desolate, sparsely populated area and remained so for decades.

In the 1970s and early 1980s, a small number of artists and local businessmen began to take an interest in the potential this urban neighborhood had. Although a number of structures were demolished, the area retained a large number of architecturally significant, historic buildings. Following the filing of an application by the Downtown Committee of Syracuse, in 1984 Armory Square was listed on the National Register of Historic Places. Forty-six buildings were included.

Today over 60 shops, upscale restaurants, and taverns line the streets of this trendy, urban area. It was the vision of several developers, such as George W. Curry, Robert Doucette, Terry Riley, and Edward Butler, in the 1980s that was key to the revitalization of the area. These developers saw an area rich with history and brimming with potential. They envisioned and began working toward developing a downtown area much like it has become—complete with luxury condominiums housing professionals and creative artists, office space, unique shops, upscale salons, fantastic bakeries, superb dining experiences, and a hip nightlife.

In addition to restaurants, bars, retail establishments, and professional office space, in 1992 the former armory building itself became the Milton J. Rubenstein Museum of Science and Technology (MOST). This impressive museum featuring an IMAX theater and planetarium is a popular draw in Upstate New York for families and people of all ages. Also located in the neighborhood is the historic Landmark Theatre, which plays host to many first-class events and shows year-round.

In the interest of continuing the development of the area, a nonprofit group known as the Armory Square Association was formed in the late 1970s. A volunteer board of directors and members continue to meet regularly and work together toward their mission of encouraging "the development and preservation of commercial and residential uses within the Armory Square district, while protecting the historic, aesthetic, and mixed-use character of this unique urban neighborhood."

In 2005, the group hired a marketing agency to develop a strong, new brand image to represent the eclectic mix of offerings in this urban area. Out of this came a new Web site, armorysq.org, to provide information about all the local businesses and happenings in the area, as well as a new logo and tagline to succinctly identify what Armory Square has become today: Live, Work and Play.

CHAPTER 1

West Jefferson Street

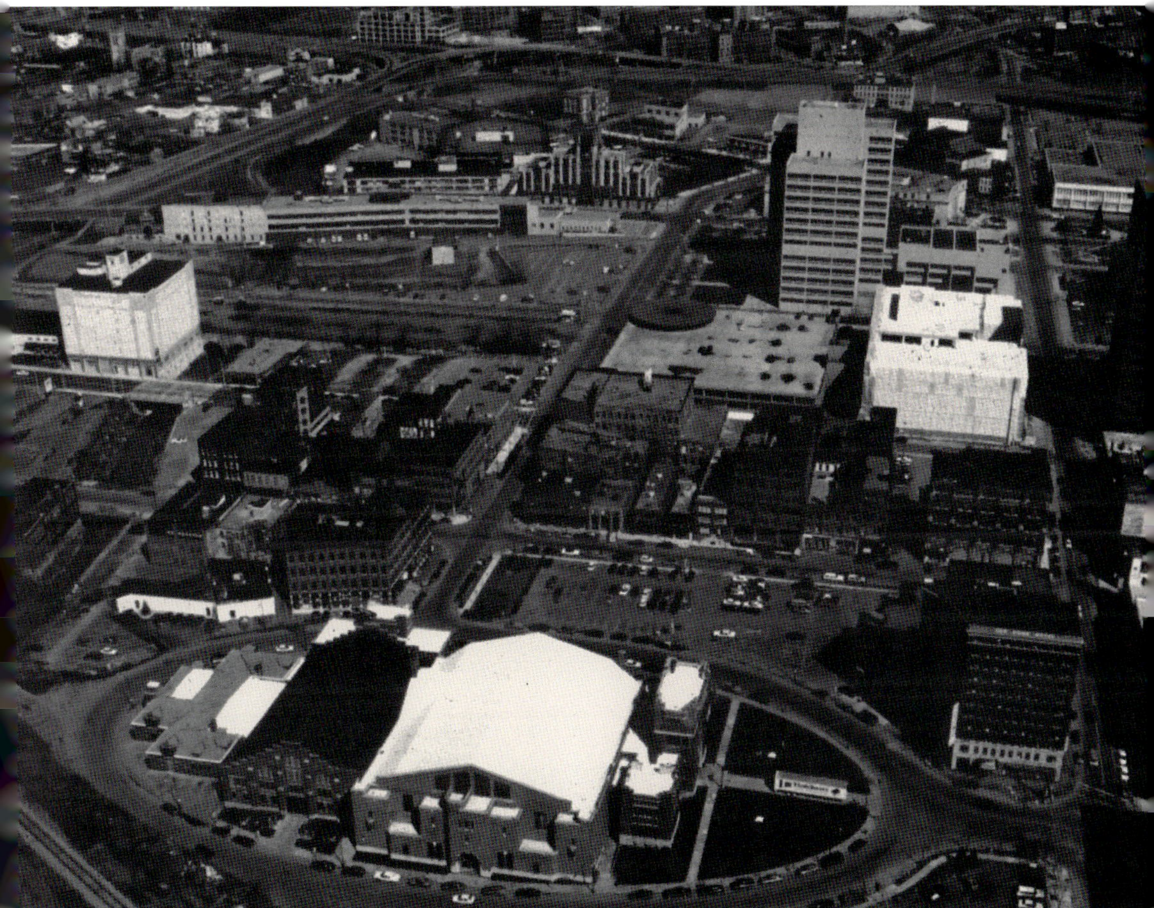

At the bottom of this aerial photograph stands the namesake for the neighborhood dubbed Armory Square—the former Jefferson Street Armory. Decommissioned in the early 1990s, the facility is now home to the Milton J. Rubenstein Museum of Science and Technology (MOST). Inside are numerous hands-on activities and displays as well as an IMAX theater.

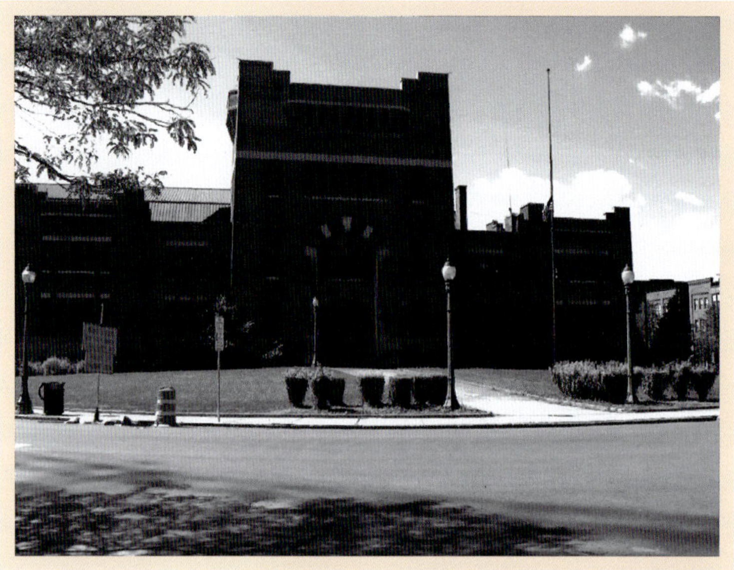

Constructed for a cost of approximately $4,000, the first Jefferson Street Armory was built in 1859. The armory building served as a drill center and social hall, also providing office space and arms depositories. The first building eventually was destroyed in a fire, and a new facility was erected at this same location in 1874. A function expressed by its medieval-castle detailing and massing, the new armory was to serve as a fortress in times of emergency. In 1880, Ulysses S. Grant delivered an address from here.

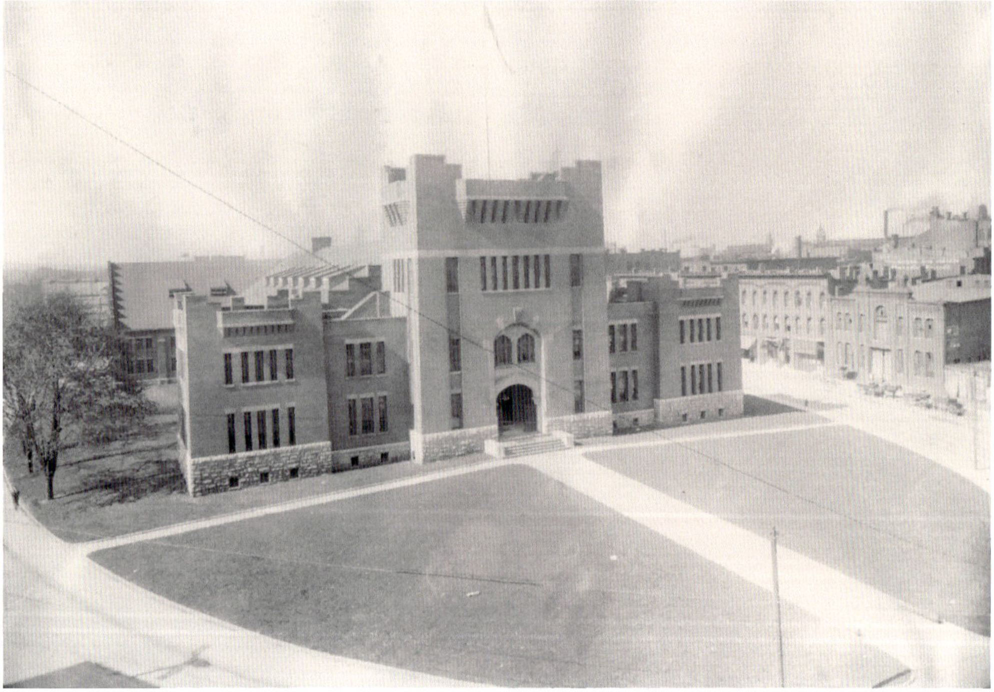

Designed by Syracuse architect Gustavus Young, the 11-story Jefferson Clinton Hotel was built in 1927 and has operated under a few different names, including the Dome Hotel (a tribute to the famous Syracuse Carrier Dome sports arena). After numerous failed ownerships, the hotel was purchased by a new owner and renovated extensively. It now operates as a luxury hotel with 60 suites and is a proud member of Historic Hotels of America.

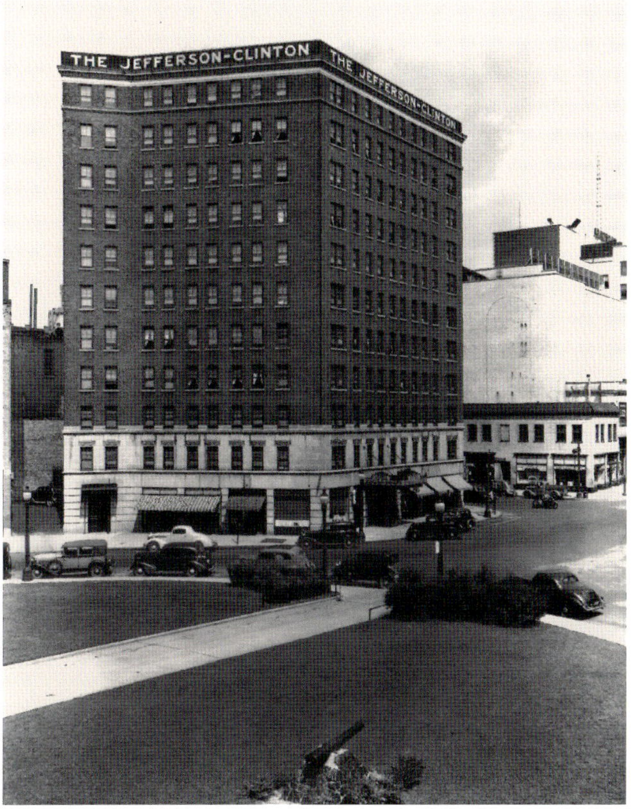

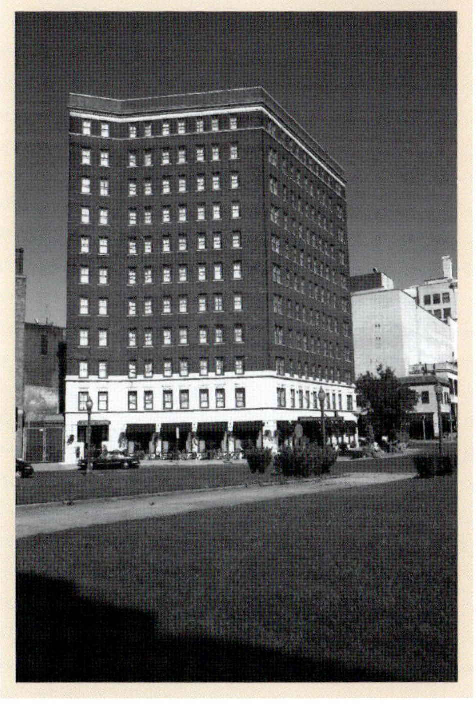

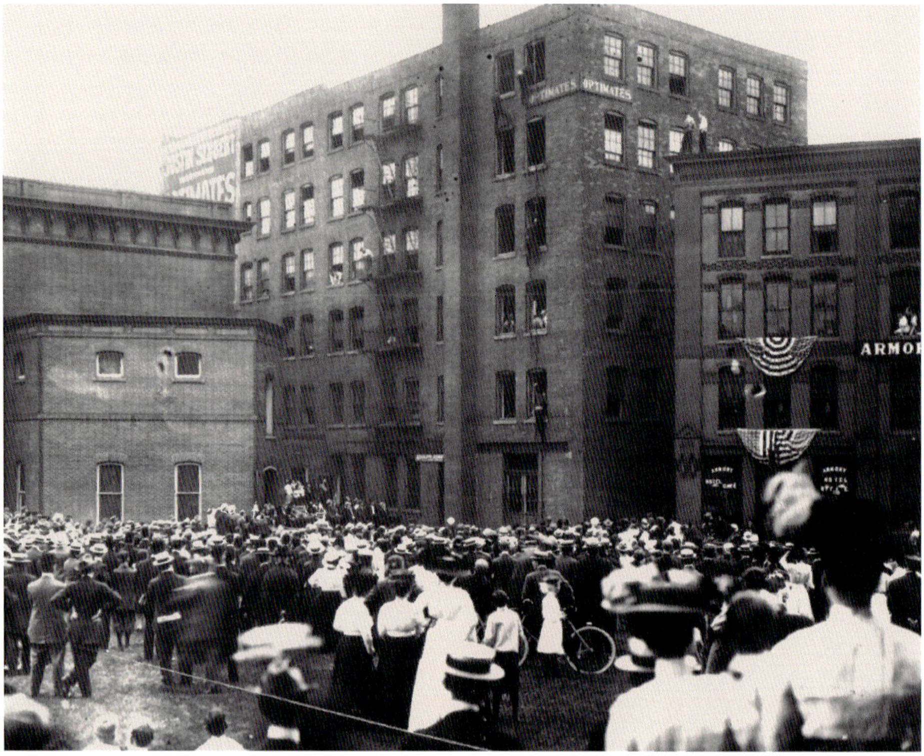

In this photograph, dated August 1910, there is a fire chief's convention in the back of the Syracuse fire engine house No. 6. People can be seen watching from the windows and rooftops of adjacent buildings, including the Armory Hotel and Café, which is no longer at that location. In the recent photograph is the construction of the Jefferson Clinton Commons in what was a parking lot. A sign of the times today, this new, environmentally friendly facility is being built with green building innovations and methods.

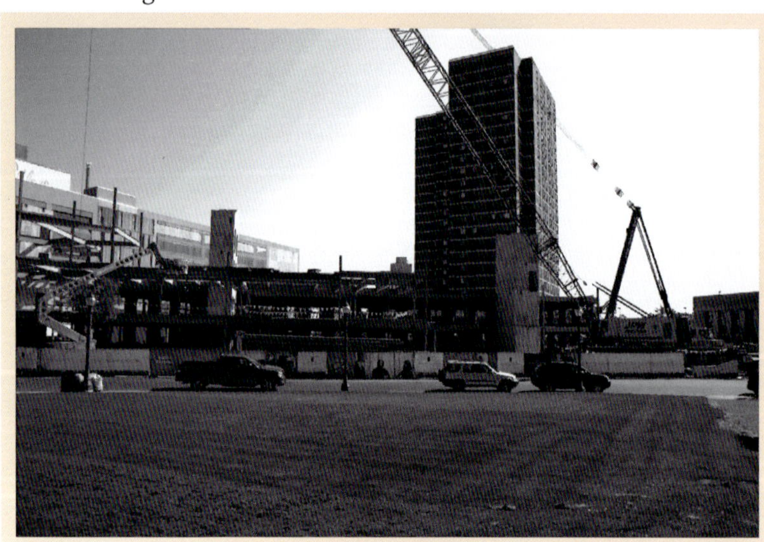

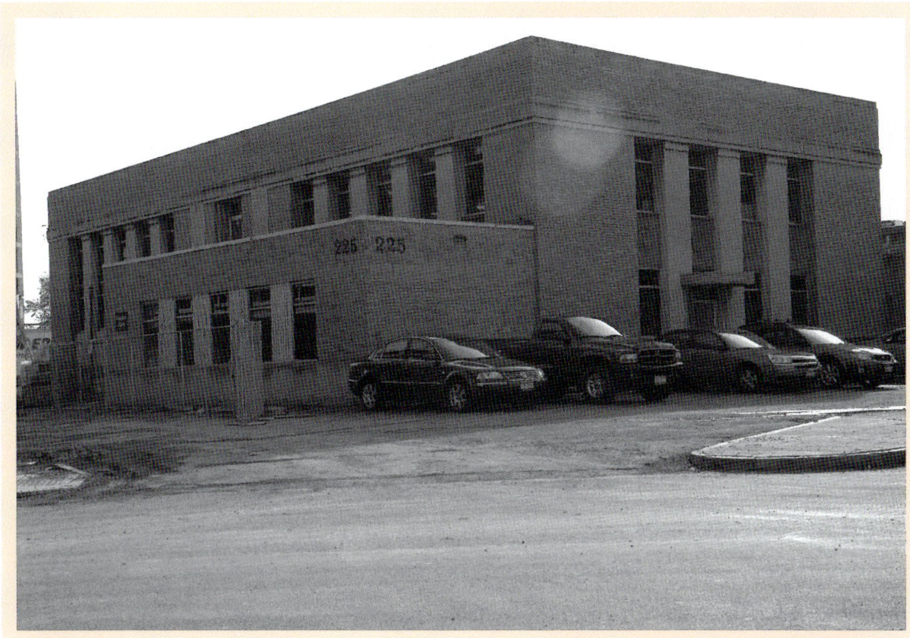

The Delaware, Lackawanna and Western Railroad (DL&W) opened its first station in the Armory Square area in 1848. The second structure seen here was built in 1941. After closing as a passenger station in the late 1950s, it was sold in 1961 and later remodeled. Since, the building has served many functions, including bus station and restaurant. Most recently, it has served as the home to a real estate appraisal company that moved there and renovated the facility in 1986.

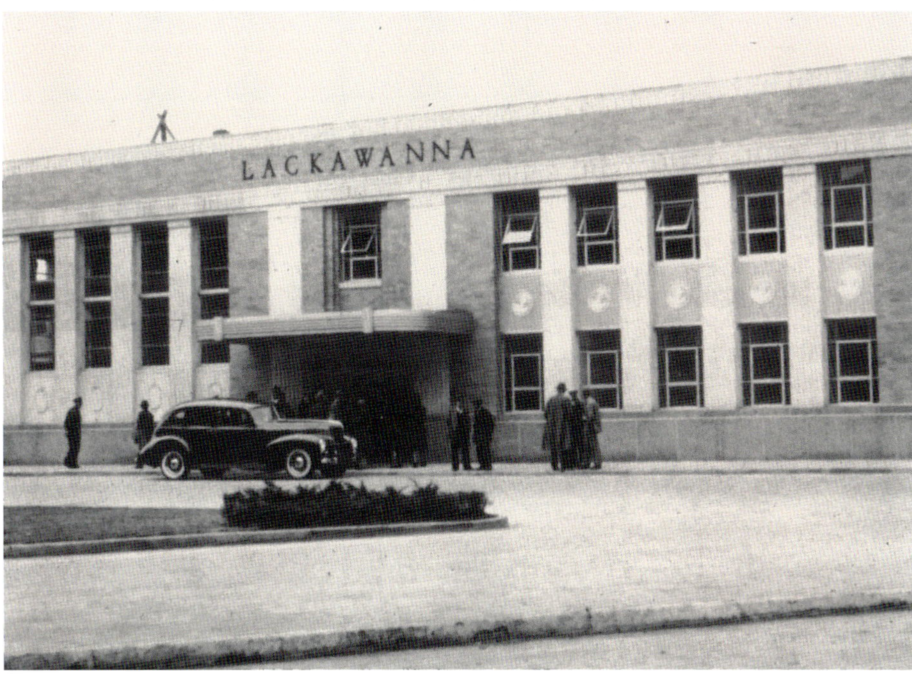

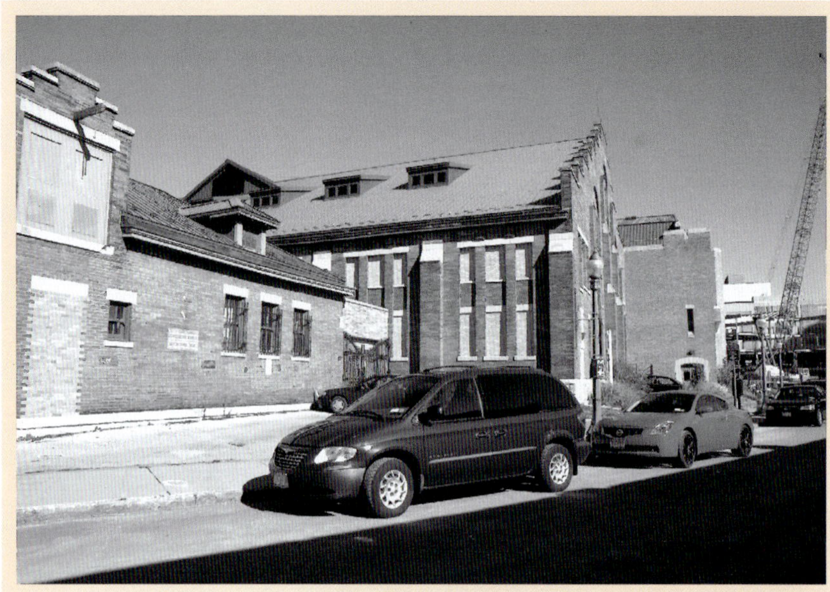

In this photograph from the early 1900s, the first DL&W passenger station behind the Jefferson Street Armory can be seen on the right. Note this was also prior to the wall being built to raise the railroads. The current picture shows the rear of the former armory, now the MOST.

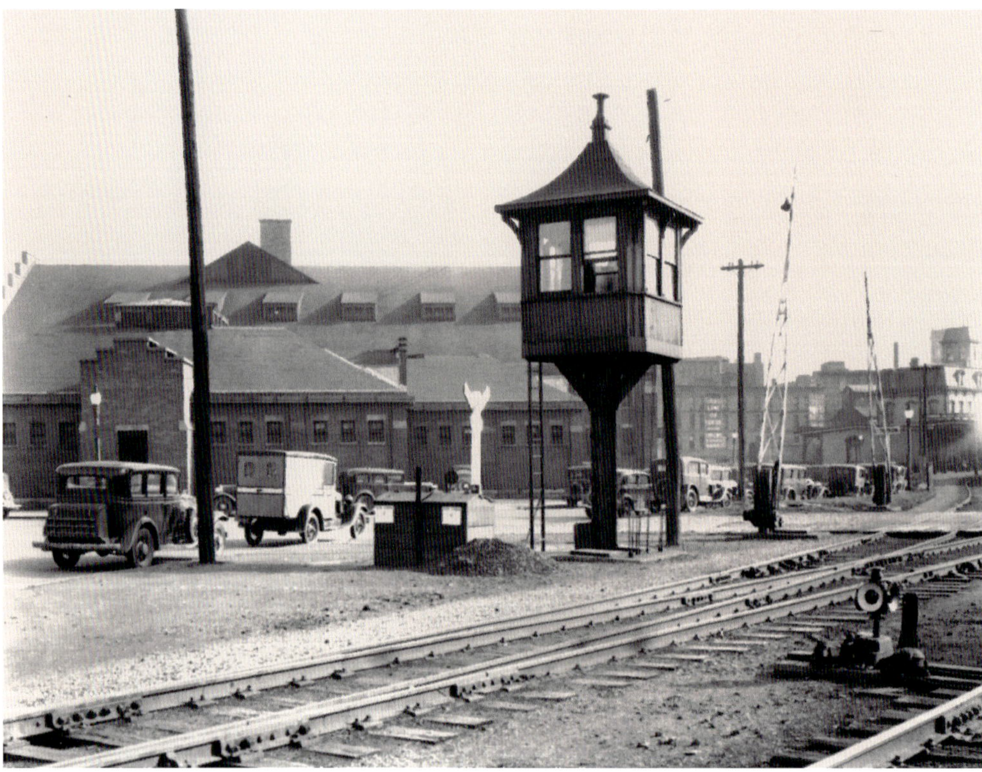

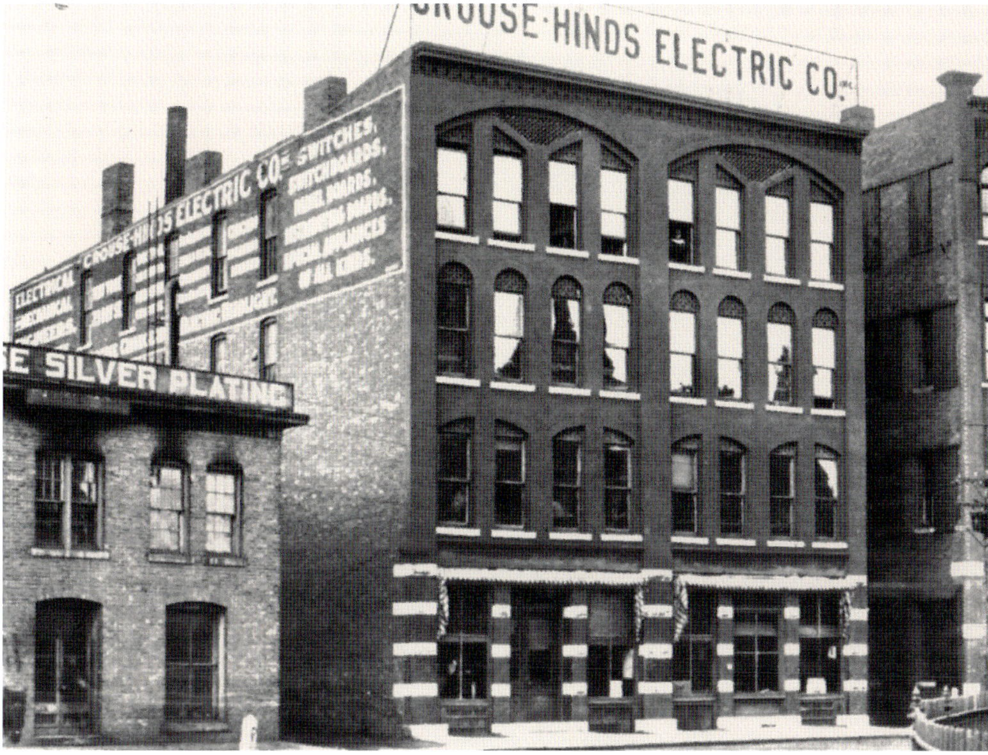

Crouse-Hinds Electric Company, a manufacturer of electrical parts, at one time operated out of this facility adjacent to the armory on West Jefferson Street near the corner of South Franklin Street. Now a worldwide company known as Cooper Crouse-Hinds, the company still maintains a manufacturing facility and headquarters in Syracuse. Today only the first floor of the original building remains, and in the fall of 2008, the Sound Garden, Syracuse's top independent music retailer, moved into the space.

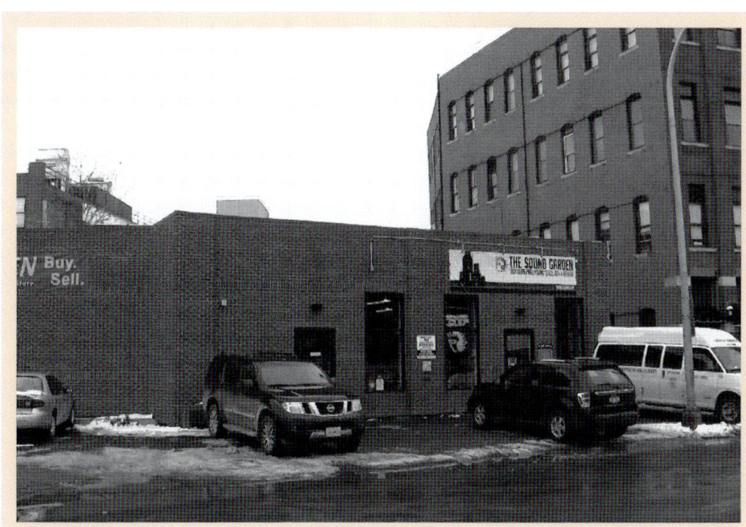

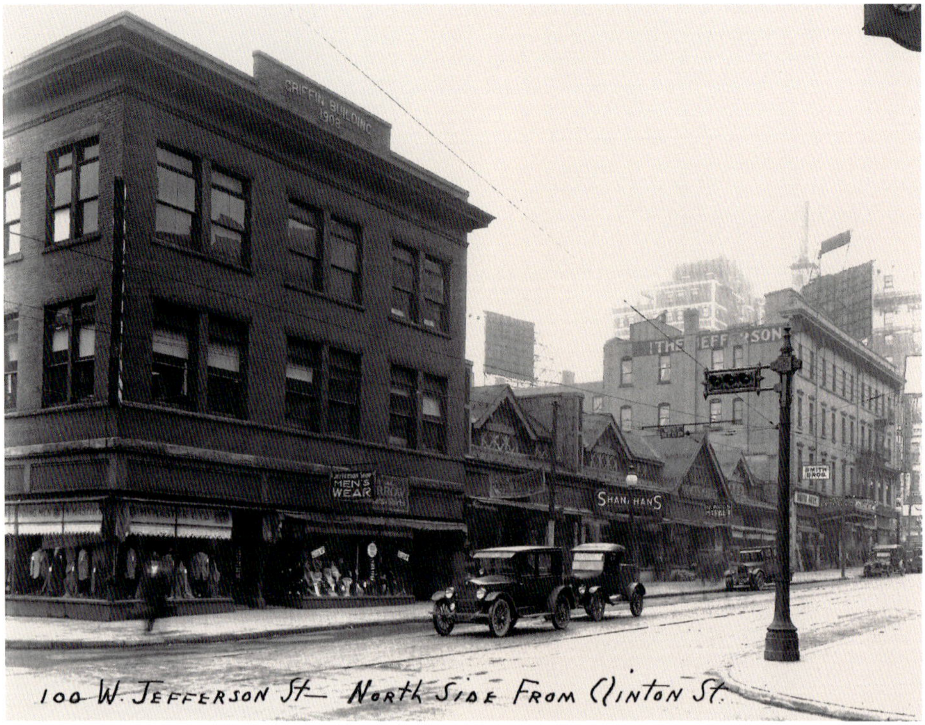

At the intersection of West Jefferson and South Clinton Streets, this photograph was taken in the early 1900s. In the Griffin Building, built in 1908, a men's clothing shop operated out of the first floor. Just up the street was a market, Smith Brothers, and the Jefferson Hotel, which remained there until the mid-1920s when it was demolished. Today located on the corner of West Jefferson and South Clinton Streets is Clark's Ale House, a well-known Syracuse pub serving a popular selection of microbrews.

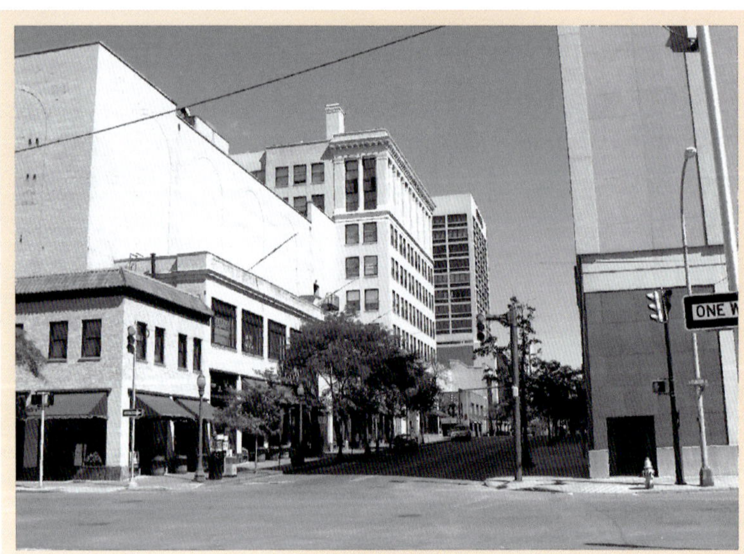

CHAPTER 2

Walton Street and Center Armory

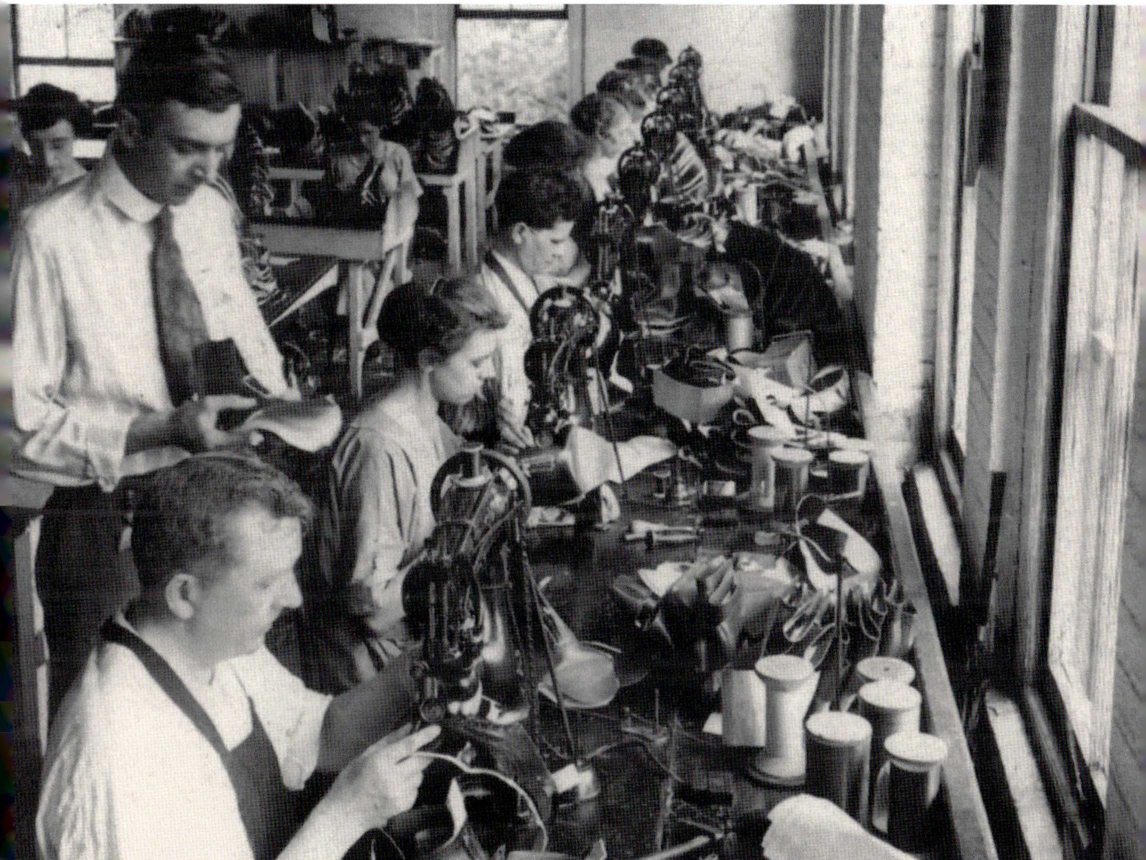

Like many great American cities, Syracuse was built on manufacturing and the railroad industry. While the growth of the railroad industry gave rise to a number of hotels downtown, many of the other buildings housed warehouses and manufacturing plants. In this photograph, employees stitch boots and shoes. The photograph is believed to be the old Gray Brothers Boot and Shoe Manufactory in the center of what is now Armory Square. (Courtesy of Robert J. Podfigurny.)

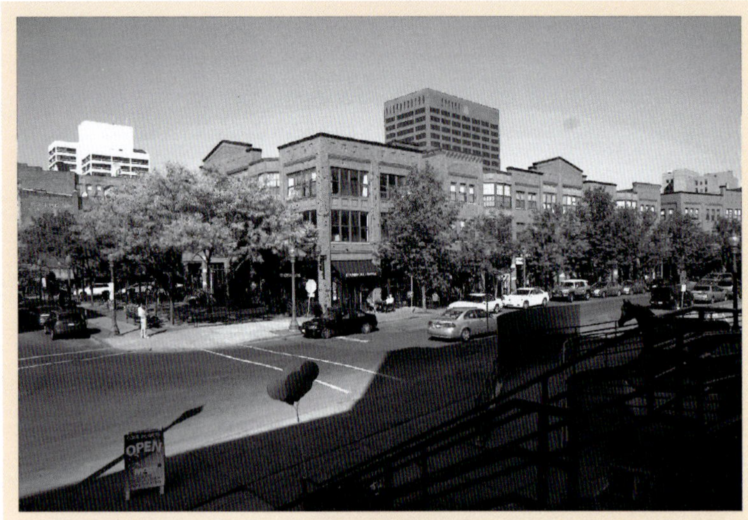

This block between Walton and West Jefferson Streets, bordered by South Franklin Street on the left, was once lined with buildings. With the decline that began to take place in the mid-20th century, these buildings were unfortunately all demolished one by one. The block remained a parking lot until the early 1990s, when Robert Doucette, one of the early visionaries to help rebuild Armory Square, developed Center Armory, a large mixed-use building featuring extensive retail space along the ground floor, with luxury townhomes above.

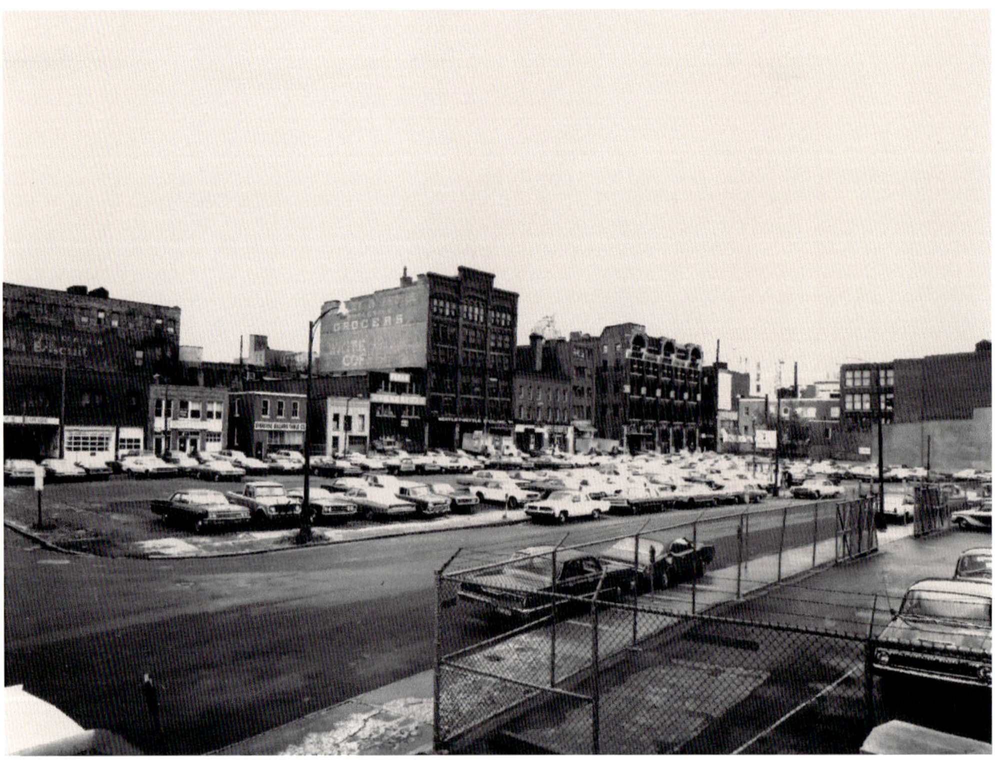

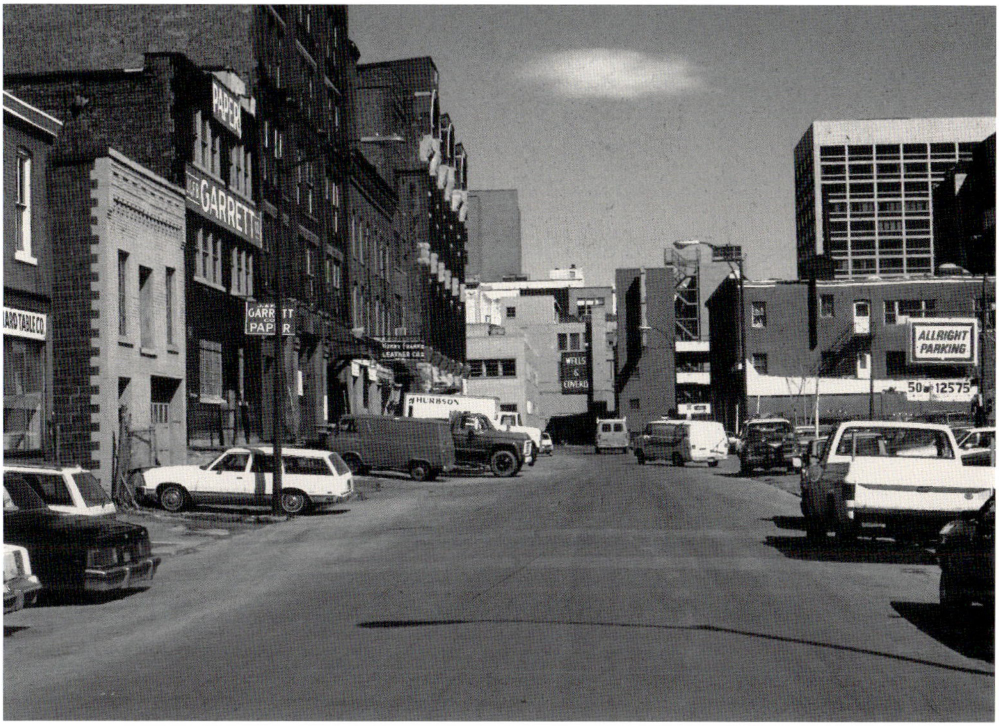

Looking east down the 100 block of Walton Street in this photograph taken in 1976, the parking lot on the right can still be seen. On the left are a number of buildings, including the Garrett Paper Company's location at the time. Today looking down the same street, the buildings on the left are all still there; however, they have changed quite a bit with the significant development that took place in the 1980s and 1990s. (Historic image courtesy of George W. Curry.)

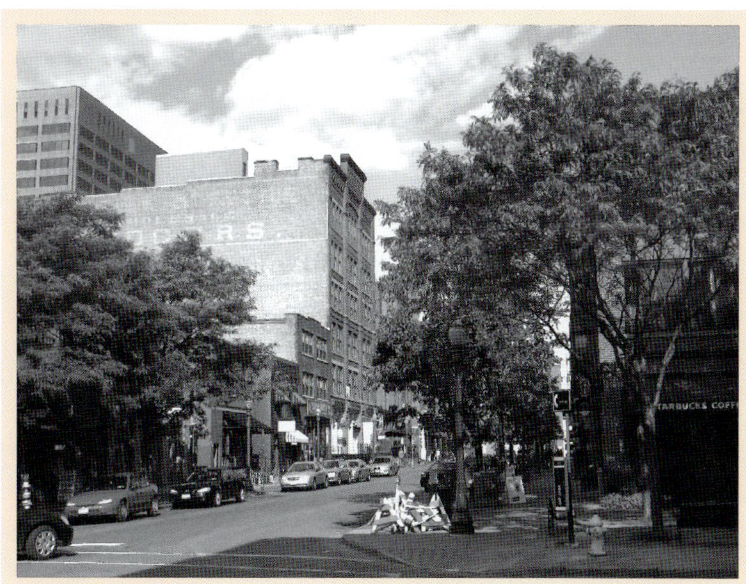

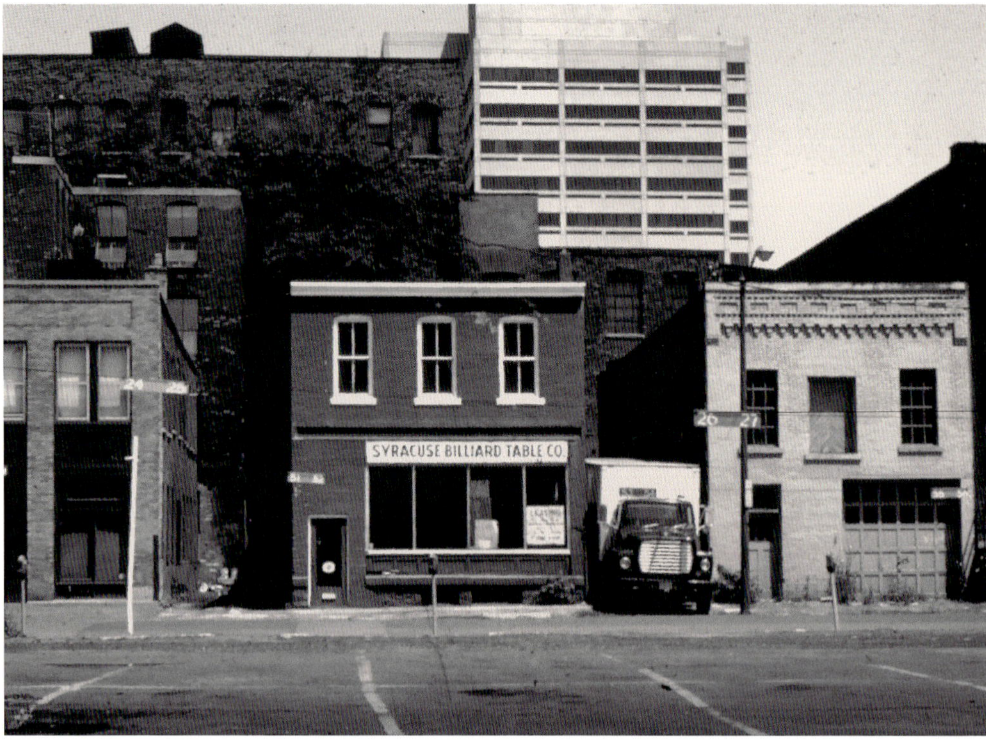

Toward the center of the 100 block of Walton Street, on the north side, sits the former home of the Syracuse Billiard Table Company. The building has since been renovated a great deal. On the ground floor is the popular Limerick Irish Pub, and the floor above provides office space to an architectural firm. (Historic image courtesy of George W. Curry.)

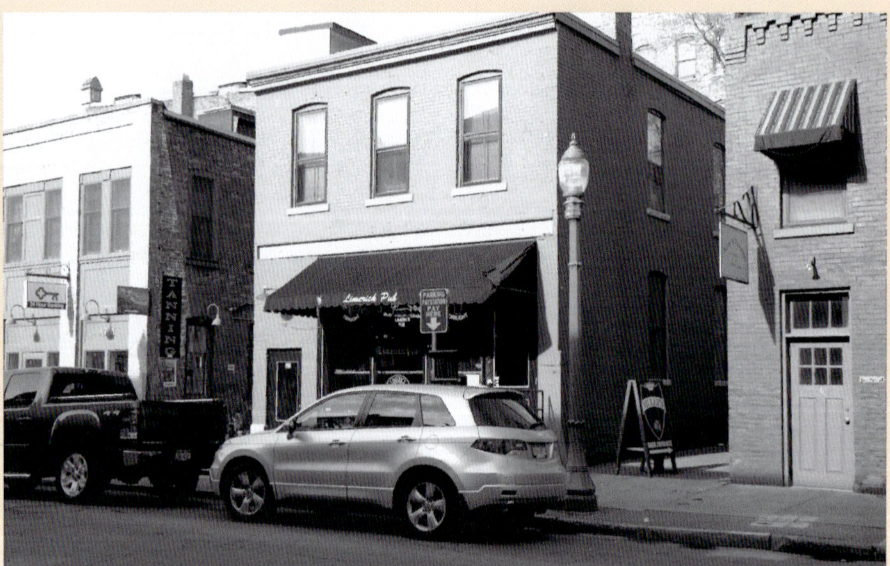

Erected in 1895, the Bentley-Settle Building was a warehouse at one time for the Bentley-Settle wholesale grocery company, which operated from 1896 to 1973. In the mid-1970s, its upper floors once provided space for Eureka Studios, a group of artists and early pioneers of the modern Armory Square. Today there are offices on the upper floors, retail on the first, and the basement is home to a very popular brewpub, the Empire Brewing Company, which manufacturers its own microbrews right on-site. (Historic image courtesy of George W. Curry.)

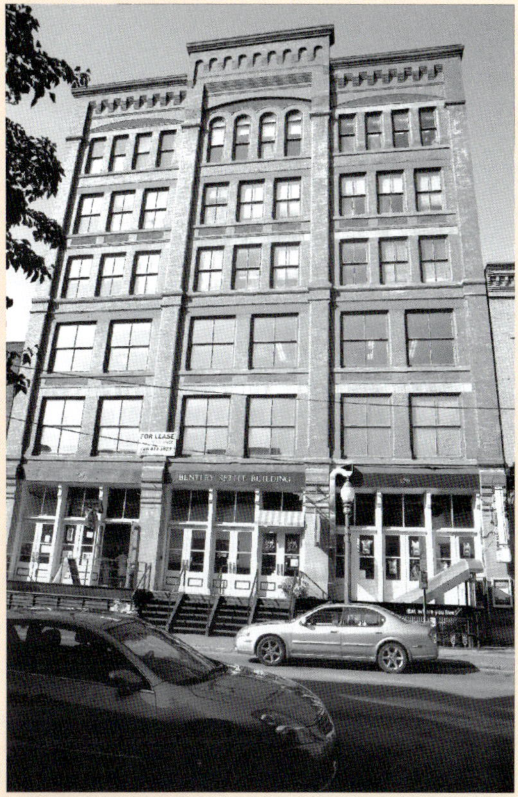

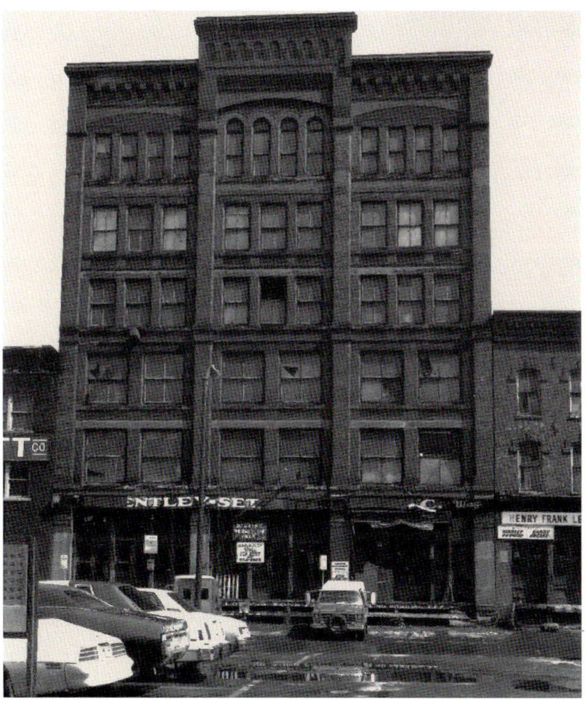

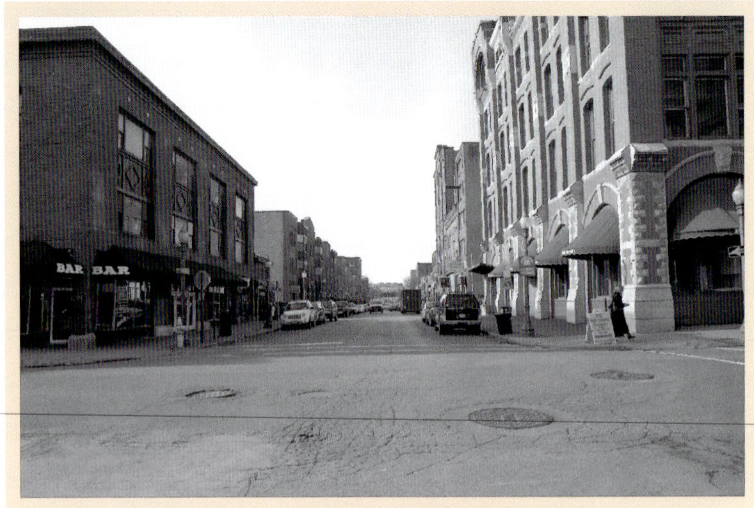

Standing at the opposite end of the 100 block of Walton Street, looking west, the former parking lot is visible on the left in this photograph from 1979. On the right, a Hurbson's Office Interior truck is backed into the loading dock for that business.

Today the Center Armory complex stands in the location of the parking lot and a nightclub is located in the Clinton Building on the left. Syracuse Suds Factory occupies the ground floor of the Neal and Hyde building on the near right.

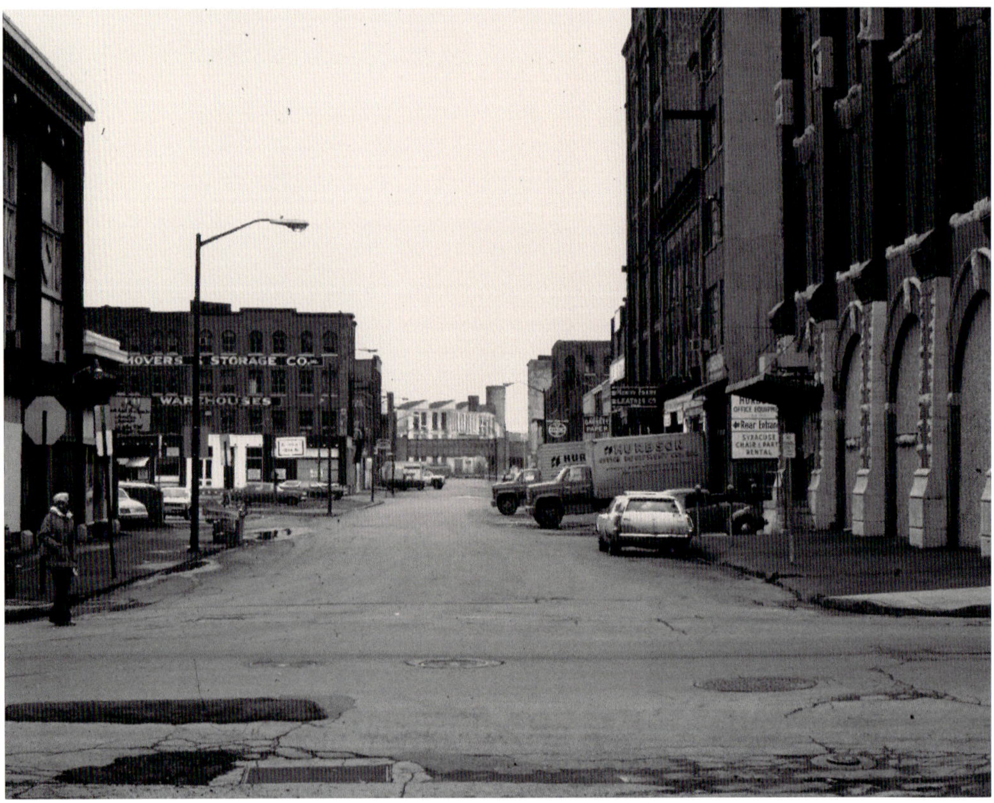

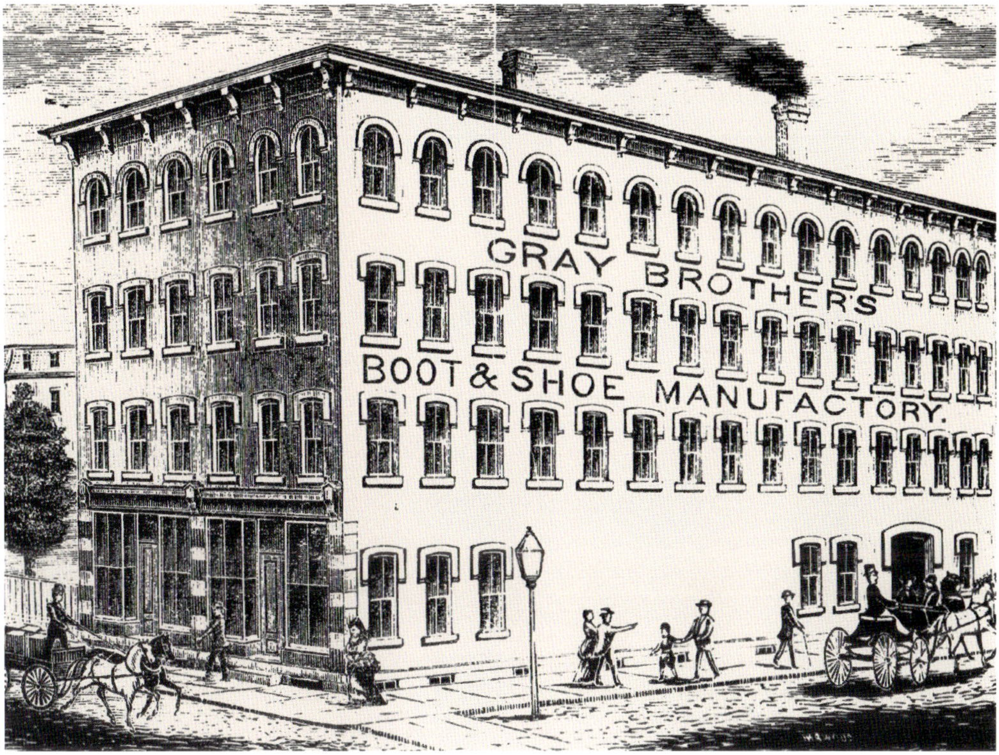

Originally built in 1873 for the Gray Brothers Boot and Shoe Manufactory, this building on the northwest corner of Walton and South Franklin Streets was later bought in the 1920s by Misener, manufacturers of circular saws. The new owners built a three-story addition, which can be seen in the contemporary photograph. Local developer RHS Holdings, LLC, has redeveloped the building into a mixed-use building featuring a popular nightclub on the first floor, with office space and luxury condominiums on the upper floors.

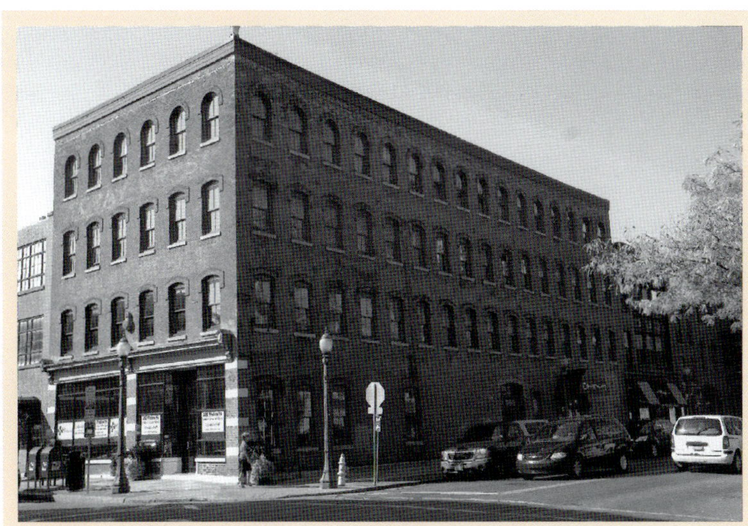

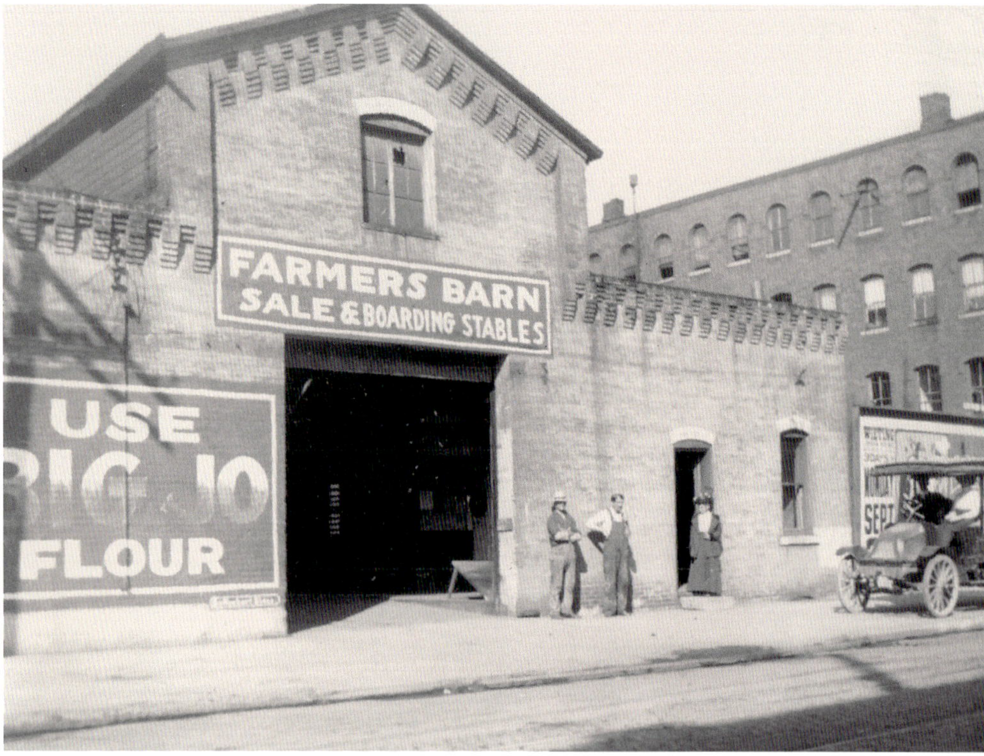

Today just to the west of the Misener building is the home of Eureka Crafts (originally Eureka Studios), the home for some of the artists and early inhabitants of present-day Armory Square. Built in 1850 and one of the oldest in the neighborhood, the building once held stables and has since been covered with aluminum sheeting. Eureka Studios may have marked the rebirth of the square with its modest beginnings in the upper floors of the Bentley-Settle Building just down the street in the mid-1970s.

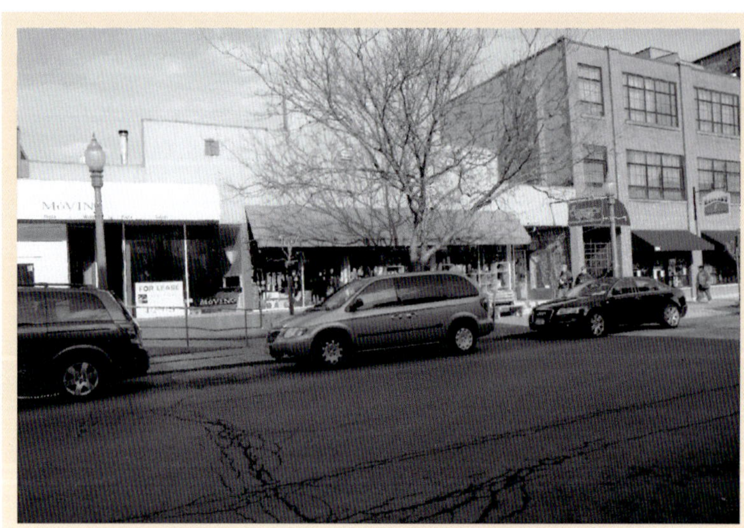

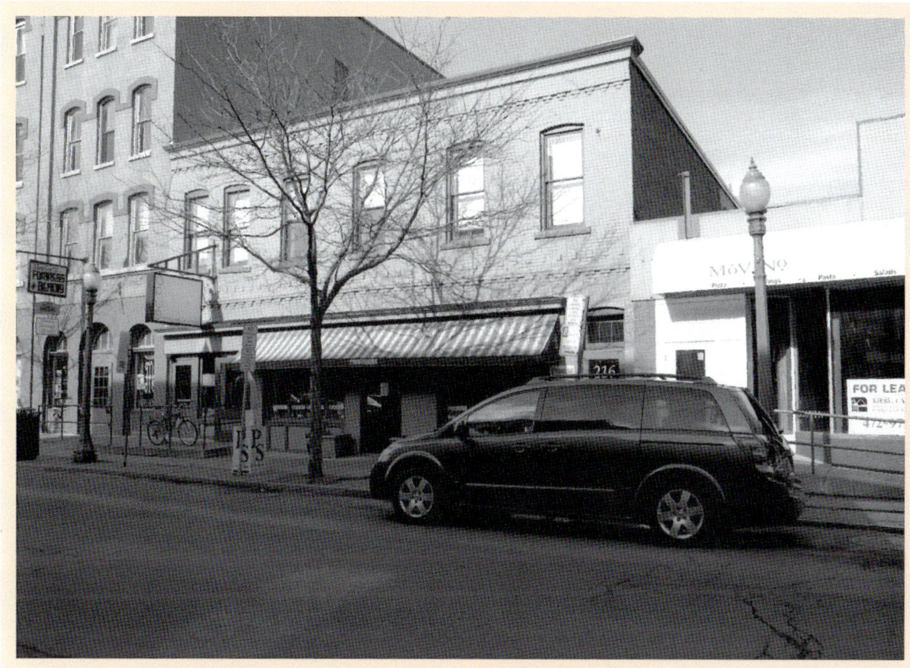

Now home to Provisions bakery and Opus Restaurant and Lounge with offices located on the second floor, this building was constructed in the 1860s as a location for stables. The historic photograph was taken in 1976 prior to extensive renovations beginning in 1987 that breathed life back into this building.

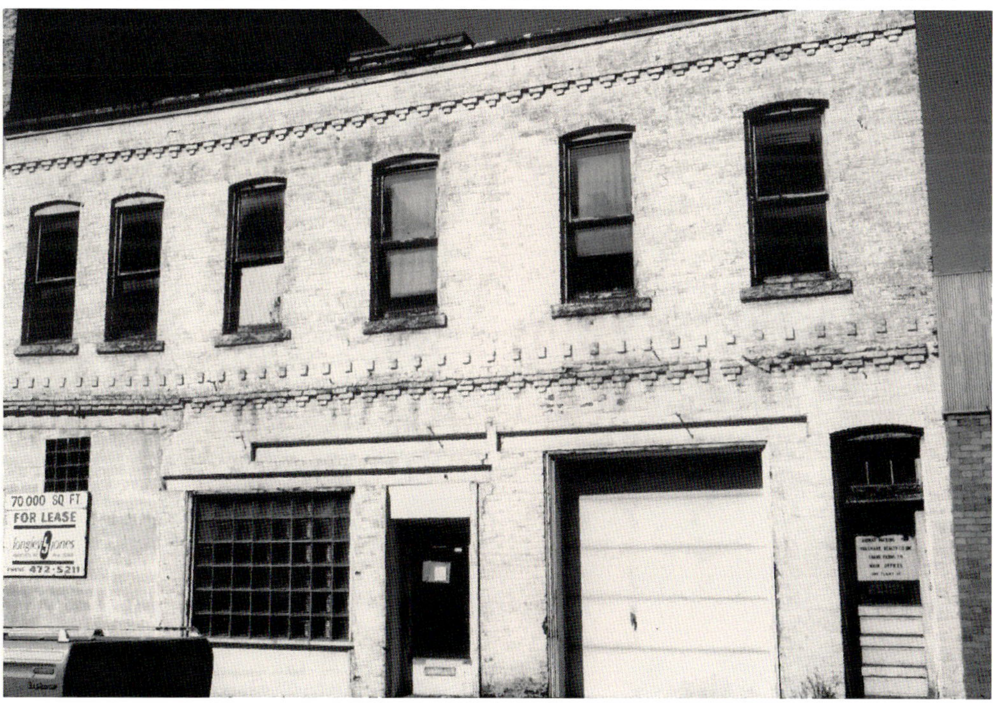

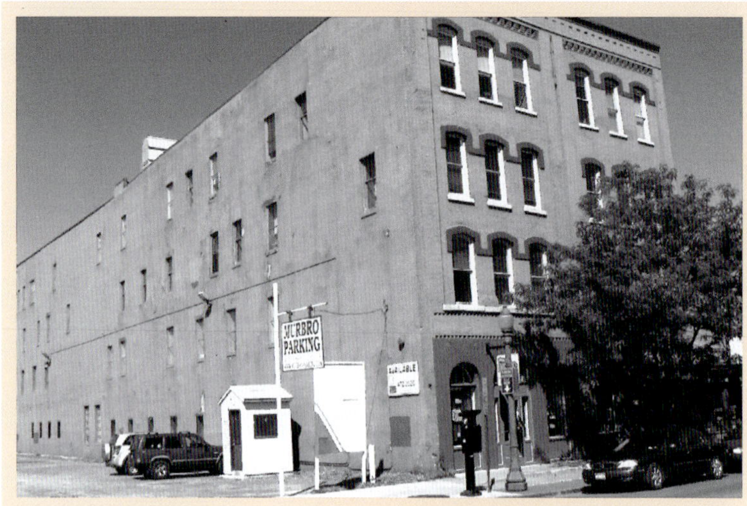

Aptly named for the former use of the site, the Mill Pond Landing Building was designed in 1878 by architect Horatio Nelson White for a wholesale grocer, A. S. Coan and Company. A fourth story was added in the late 1800s, and for much of the 20th century, the building served as a warehouse for Lerman Carpet Corporation, as can be seen in this photograph from 1976. The building was rehabilitated in 1988–1989 to offer space for service industries.

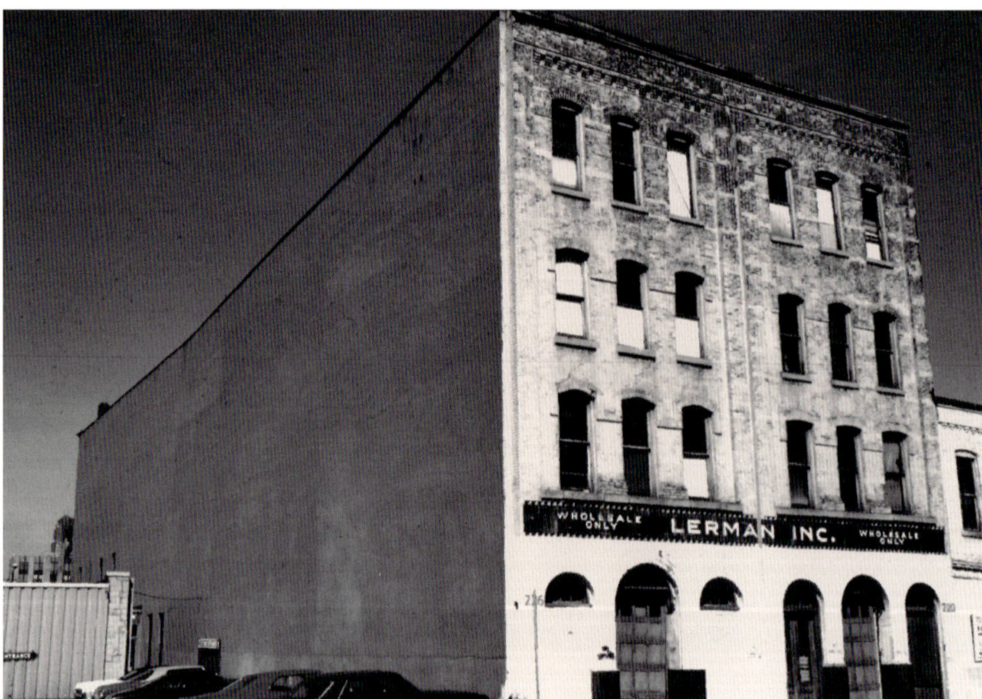

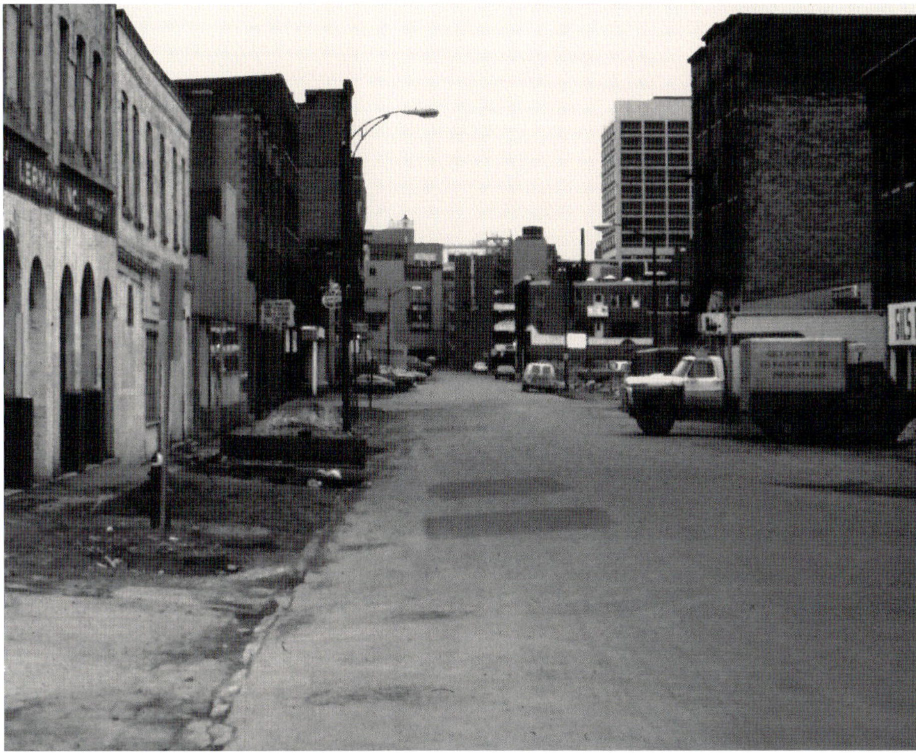

Desolation is the first word that may come to mind when looking at this photograph from 1976, prior to the rehabilitation of the Mill Pond Landing Building and the 200 block of Walton Street. Today many vehicles can be seen vying for parking spots in Armory Square. Parking is a major topic of conversation in and around Armory Square today. But talk to the early developers who invested in this area in the 1980s, and they will tell of a time when they dreamed of this problem. (Historic image courtesy of George W. Curry.)

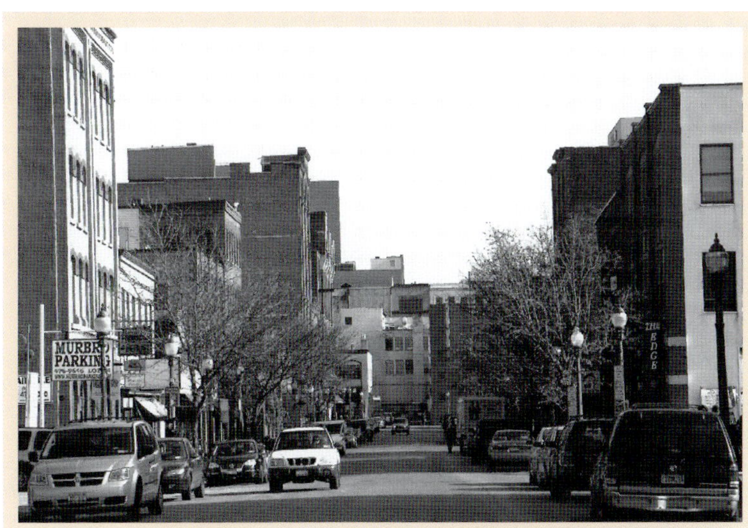

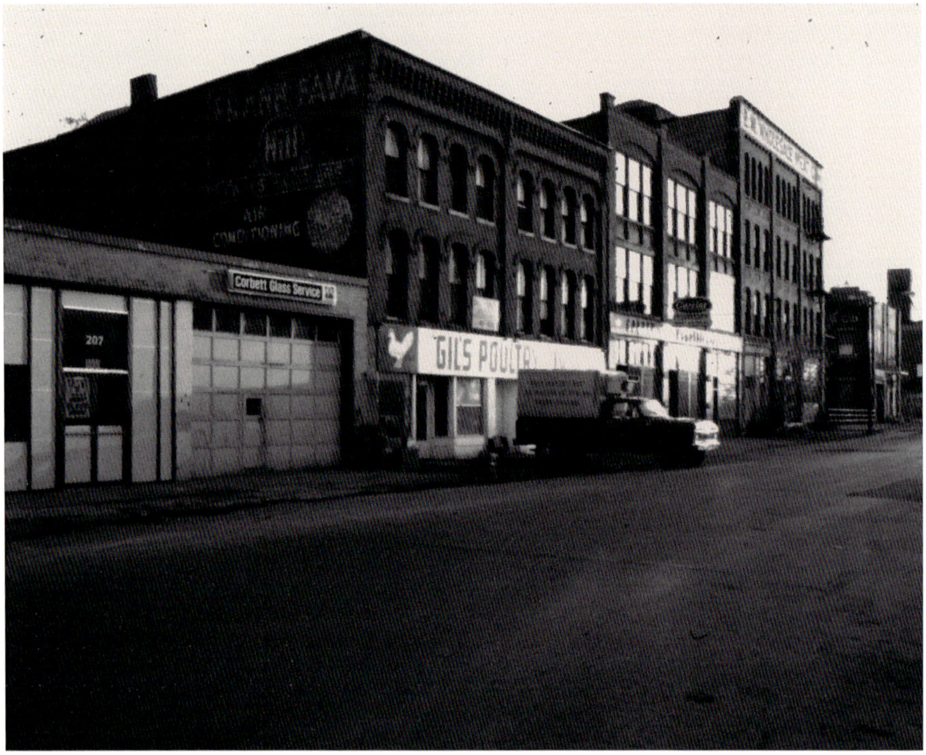

Once known as the "Chicken Building" because of its past as a chicken packinghouse, the building in the center was constructed around 1872. It is believed it may have at one time served as a warehouse for the Crouse-Hinds Electric Company, as there is an underground tunnel connecting it to the former Crouse-Hinds building located behind it. Renovations began in 1988, and today the building serves as another mixed-use facility with retail, restaurant, and office space. (Historic image courtesy of George W. Curry.)

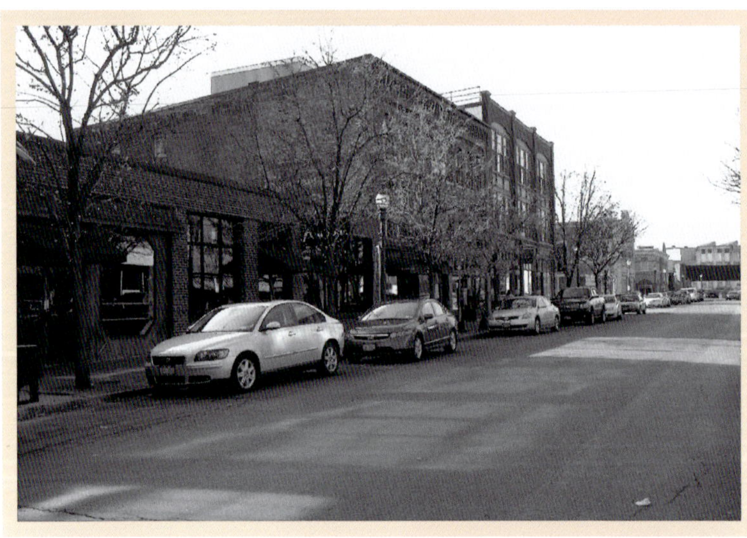

CHAPTER 3

South Franklin and West Washington Streets

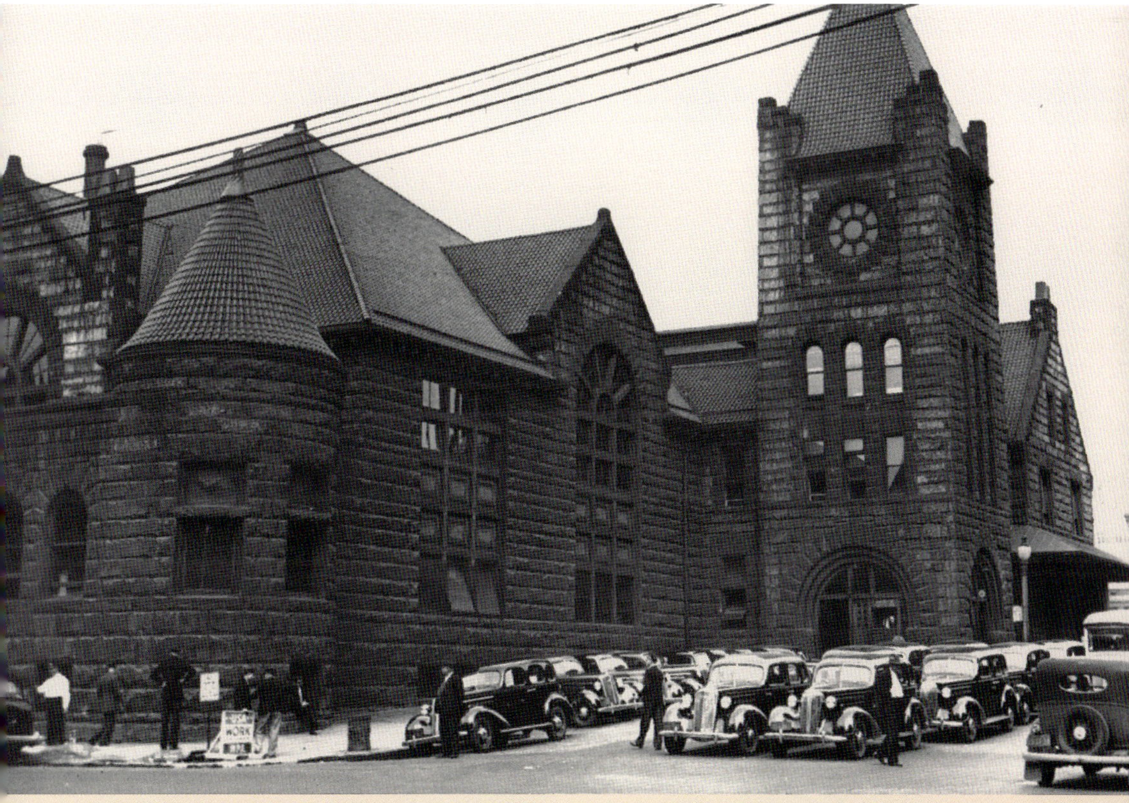

The Armory Square neighborhood was at its peak when the railroad industry was in its heyday, as can be seen in this photograph of the New York Central Railroad (NYCRR) station in the early 1900s. Today, while Armory Square is in the midst of a lengthy revival, this very location will soon be the site of yet another large development.

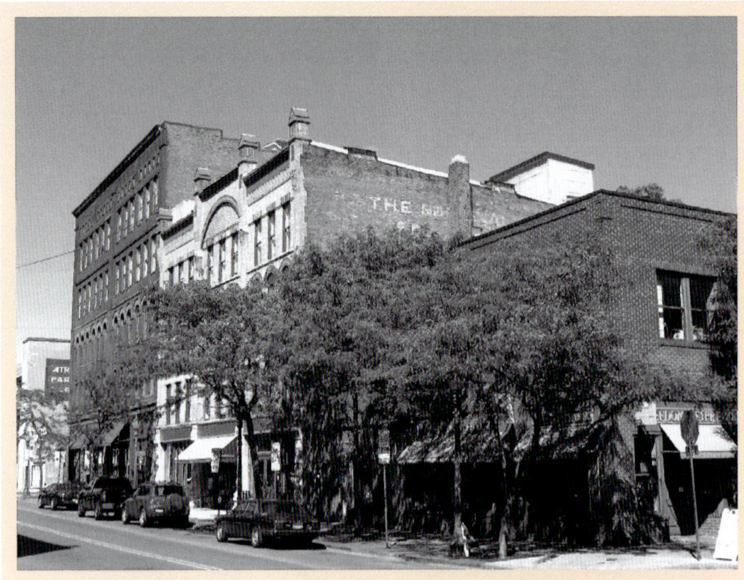

One of several printing shops in Armory Square once was located in the historic Labor Temple building located in the center of these photographs. Built in 1887 by members of the well-known, local Crouse family, this was originally known as the Crouse Building. It later became the house of a number of labor unions and took on the name Labor Temple building after 1927. It was the first building in Armory Square to be rehabilitated adhering to federal standards.

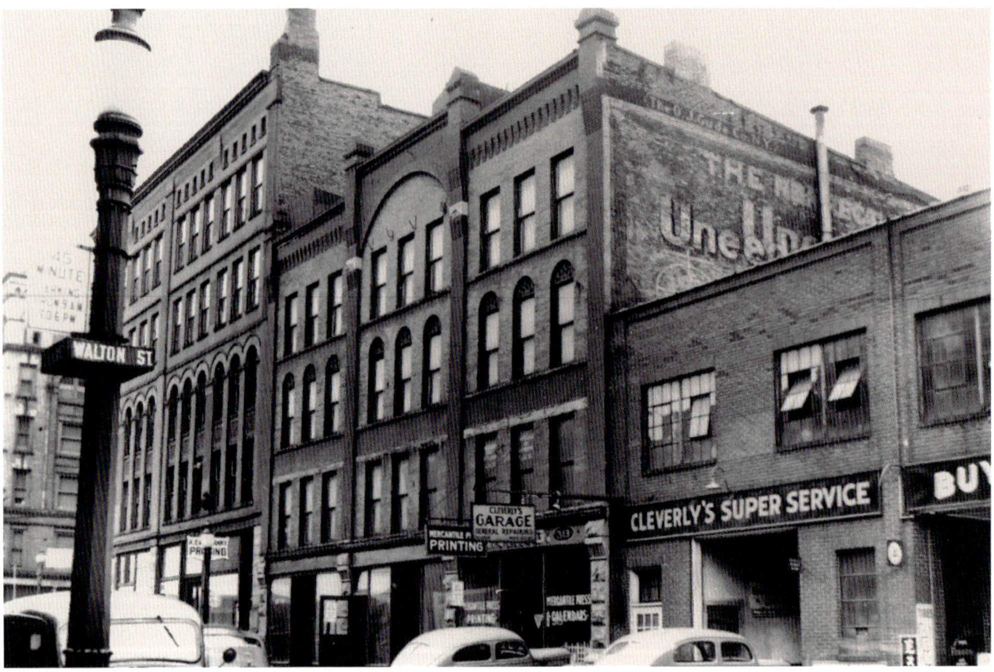

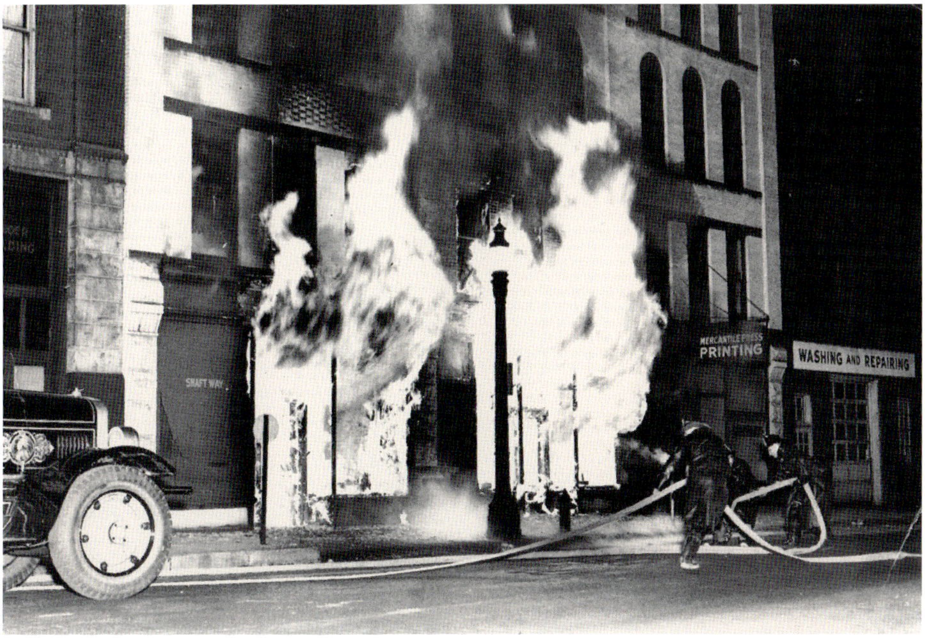

A severe fire ravaged the Labor Temple in 1948, seen in this dramatic historic photograph. Most recently, the building was one of the first rehabilitation projects in the new Armory Square neighborhood when, in 1984, Armory Square pioneers George W. Curry and Robert Doucette partnered to begin development. The pair successfully convinced a local, trendy restaurant, Pastabilities, to relocate in its ground floor. The eatery and facility continue a prosperous relationship to this day.

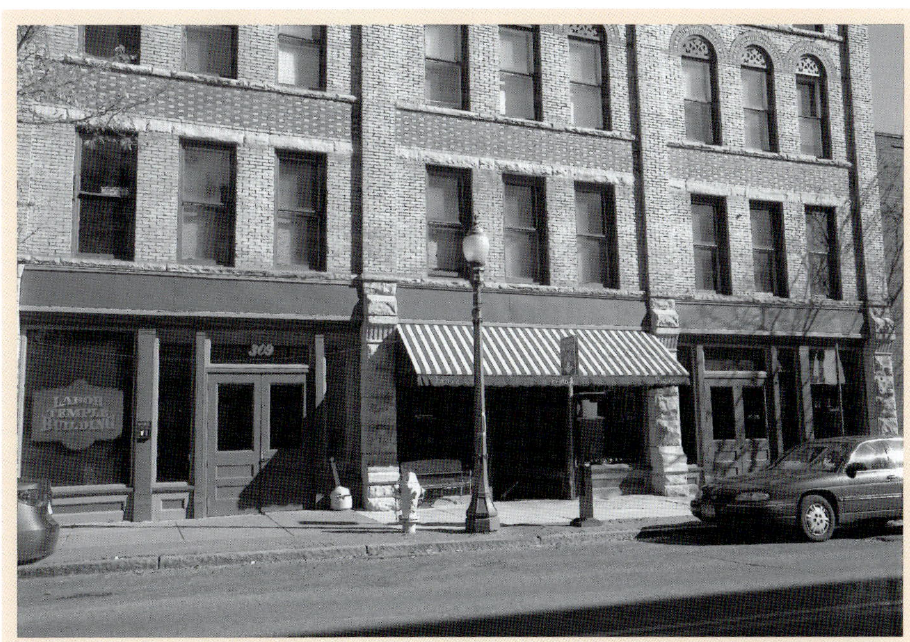

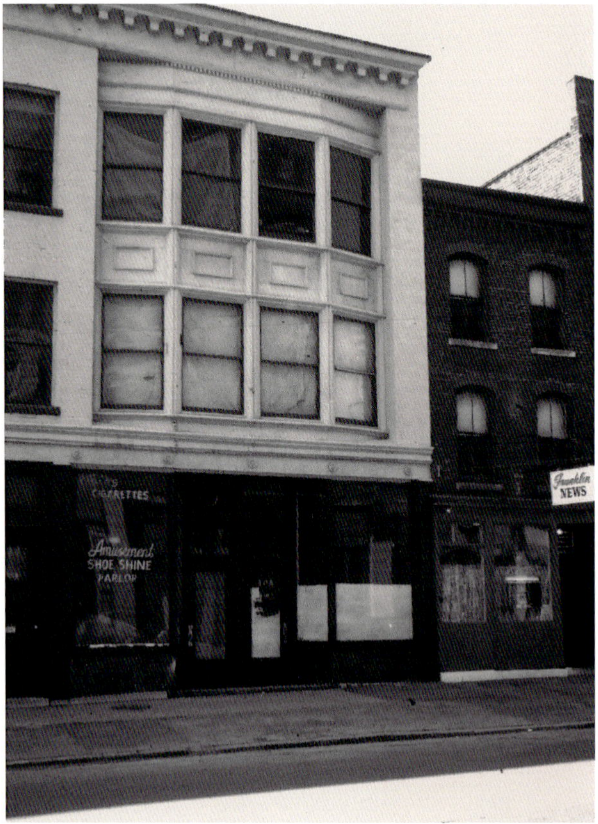

In this historic prerevival photograph from the 1970s, a shoe-shine parlor and one of several area adult bookstores can be seen. The building, located just across the street from the Labor Temple, is now home to one of Syracuse's most popular bread shops, Pasta's Daily Bread.

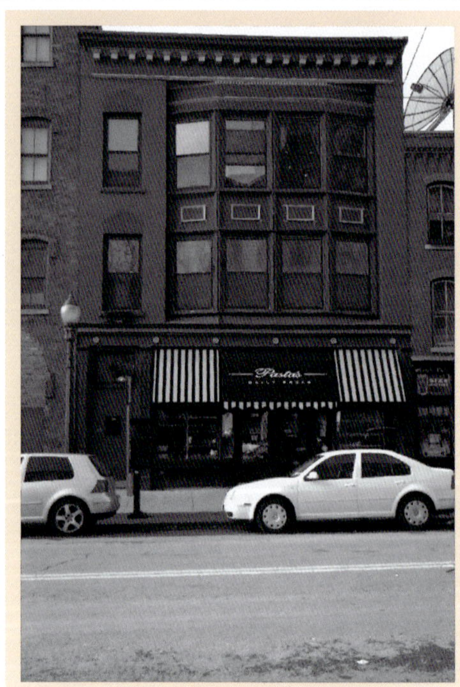

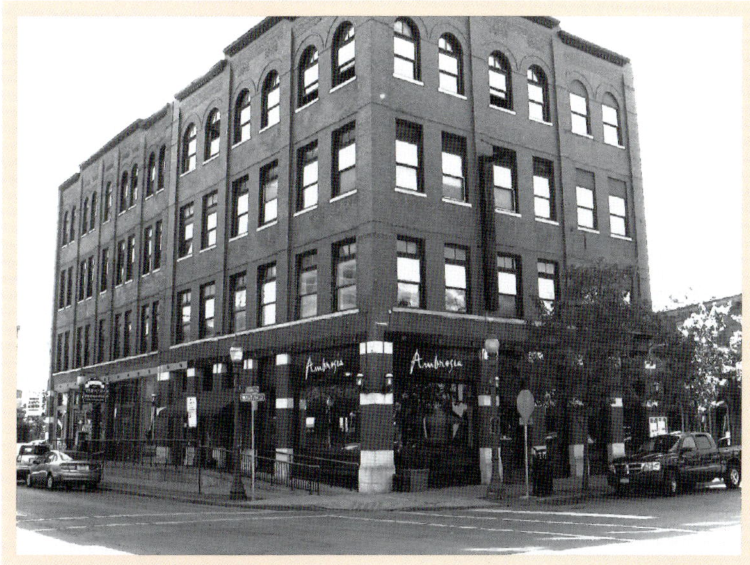

Known as the Hall-McChesney Building after the publishing, printing, and bookbinding firm that first occupied it, this block was built in two sections starting around 1897. This building maintains the distinction of being the first among many to be purchased for new uses at the start of the neighborhood revitalization. Bought by Edward Butler in the 1970s, the building houses a restaurant/nightclub with lofts above. Butler was the first president of the Armory Square Association. The association dubbed the area Armory Square in the early 1980s.

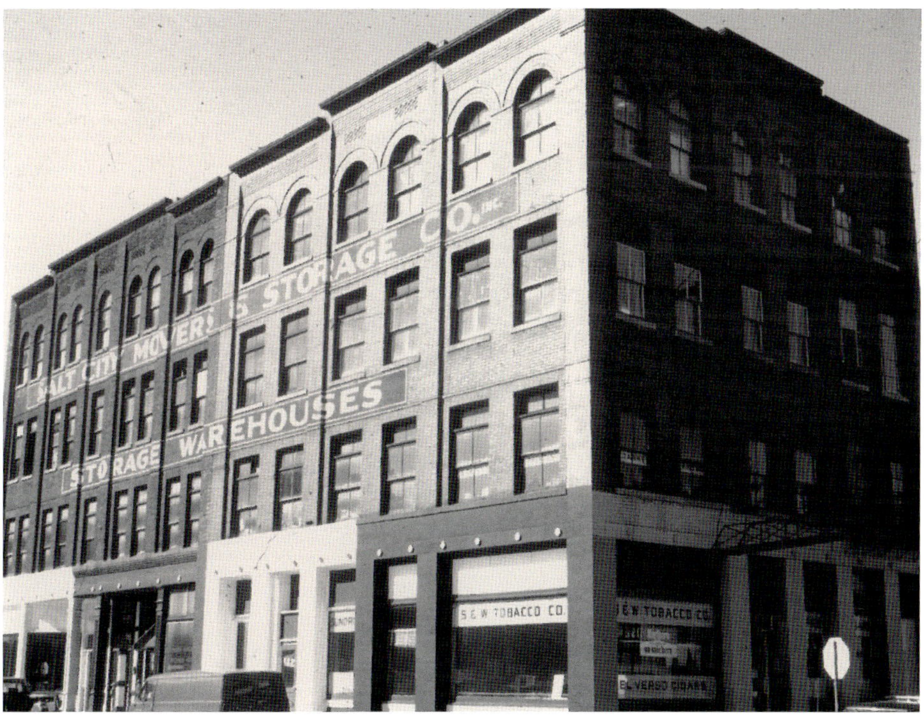

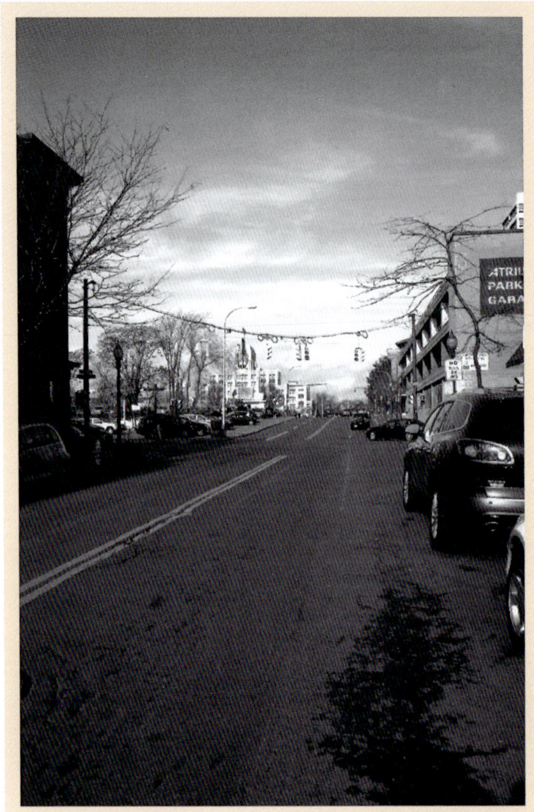

The 1869 NYCRR station and the DL&W station brought significant traffic through Armory Square beginning in the 1870s. With so many visitors and railroad employees, a great number of hotels were needed in the vicinity. Two of the many can be seen here: the Hotel Crown and the Lennox Hotel (on the right). A parking lot is on the site of the former station to accommodate today's preferred means of transportation, and a parking garage is on the site of the Lennox Hotel.

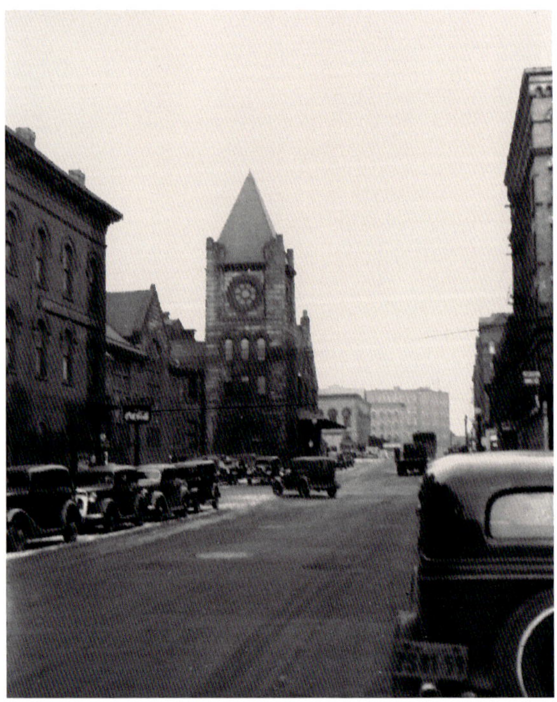

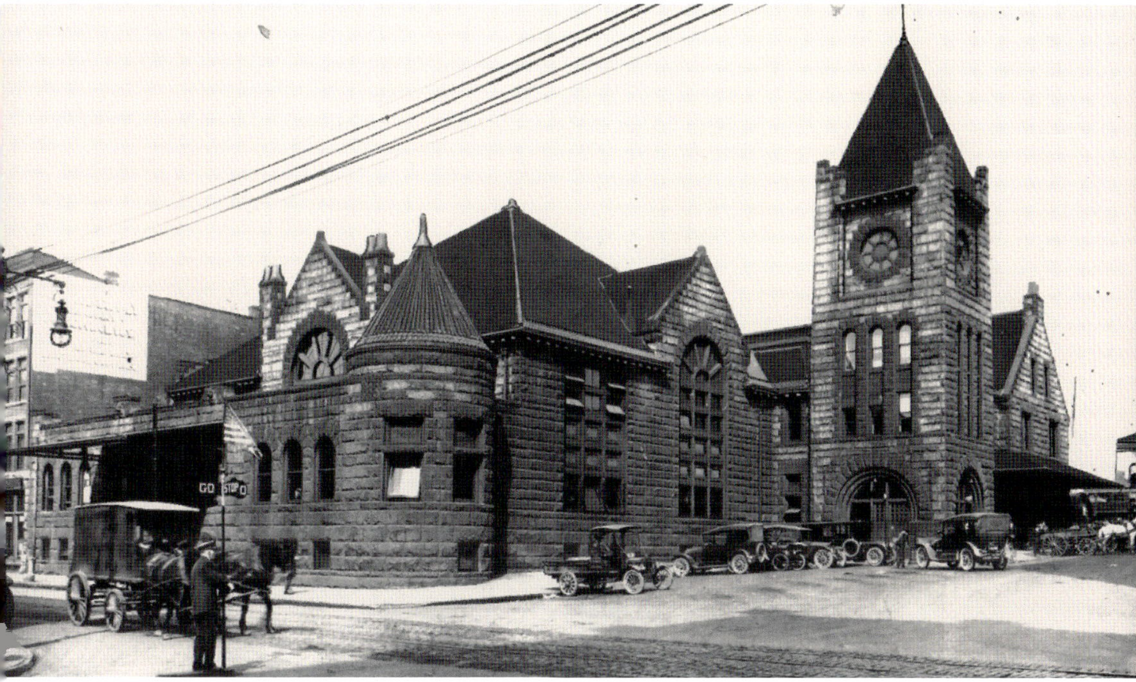

In this historic photograph, taken prior to the photograph on page 31, earlier and fewer automobiles can be seen. Note the need for a person to control a stop-and-go signal at the corner of West Fayette and South Franklin Streets. While Armory Square may no longer be a stop on the railroad transit systems, it has recently become a growing destination for both travelers and central New Yorkers. Two new hotels will soon be built on this site to offer more lodging accommodations in the square. (Contemporary image courtesy of Schopfer Architects/RHS Holdings, LLC.)

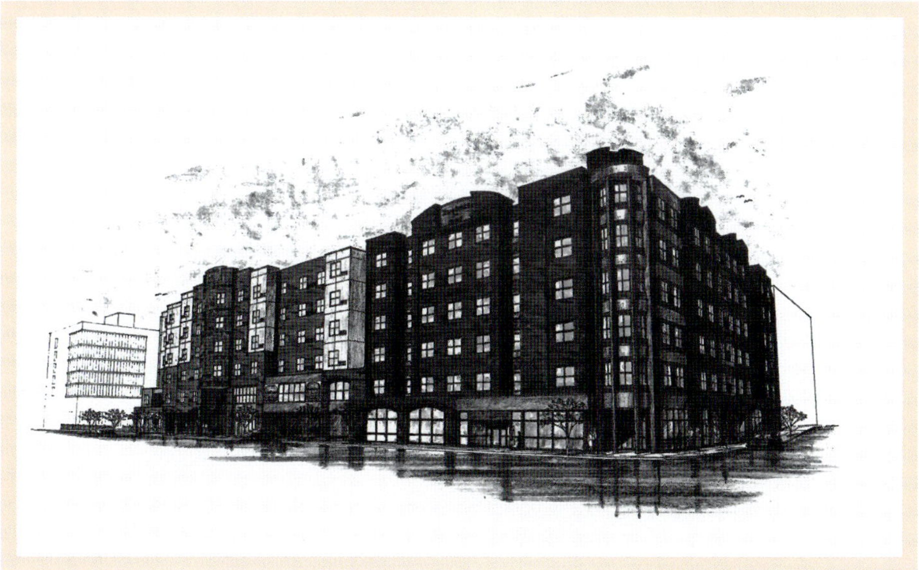

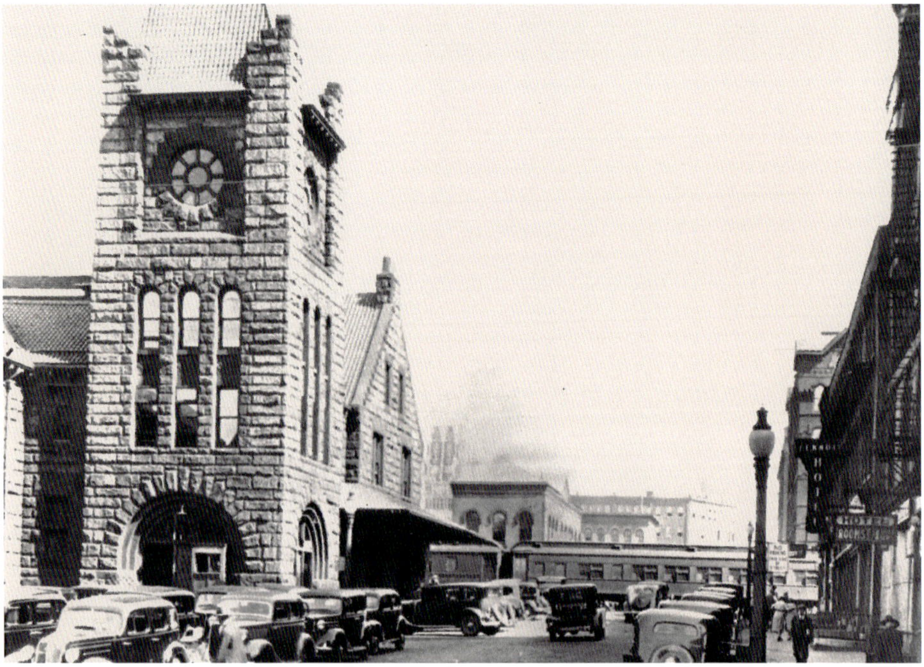

A sign for the Lennox Hotel can better be seen on the right in this historic photograph. After the hotel was demolished on this block, in 1956–1957 a successful downtown department store, E. W. Edwards, constructed a parking garage. The garage is still in operation today, although it is now named the Atrium Parking Garage.

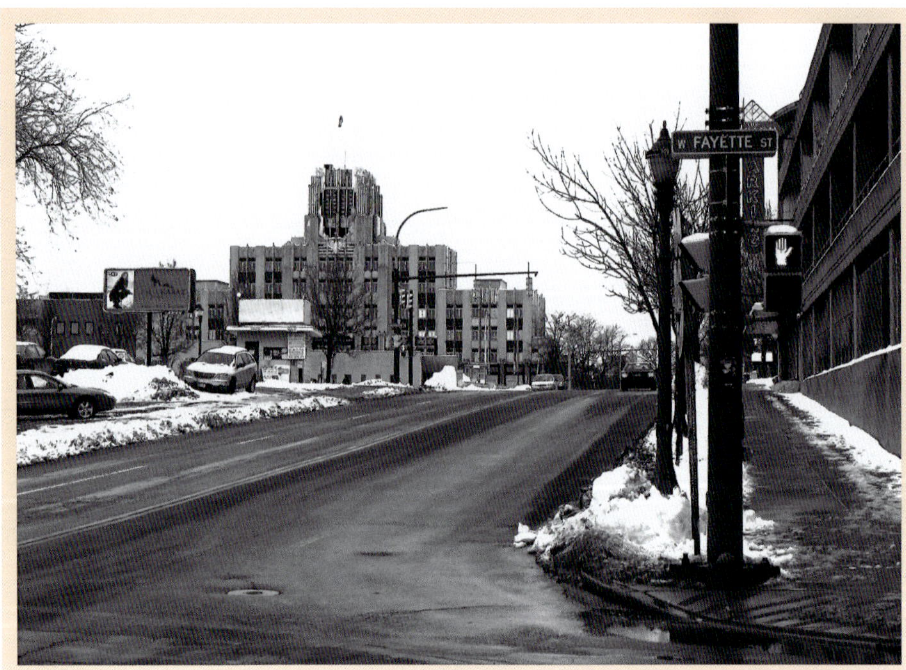

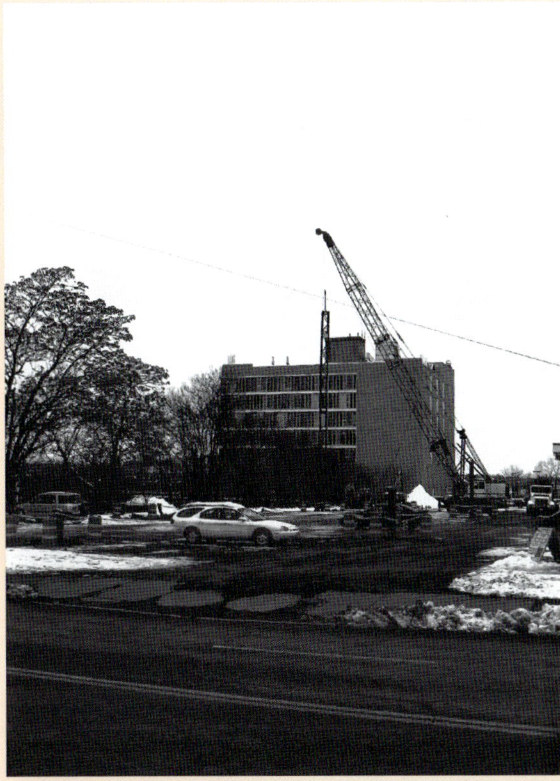

Built in 1869, the second NYCRR station stood on South Franklin Street at the corner of Washington Street. After the relocation of the NYCRR in 1936 to elevated tracks just north of Erie Boulevard, parking lots were constructed on this site. In the background, what was once a furniture warehouse is now a Syracuse University building—aptly named the Warehouse—connecting the campus to downtown Syracuse.

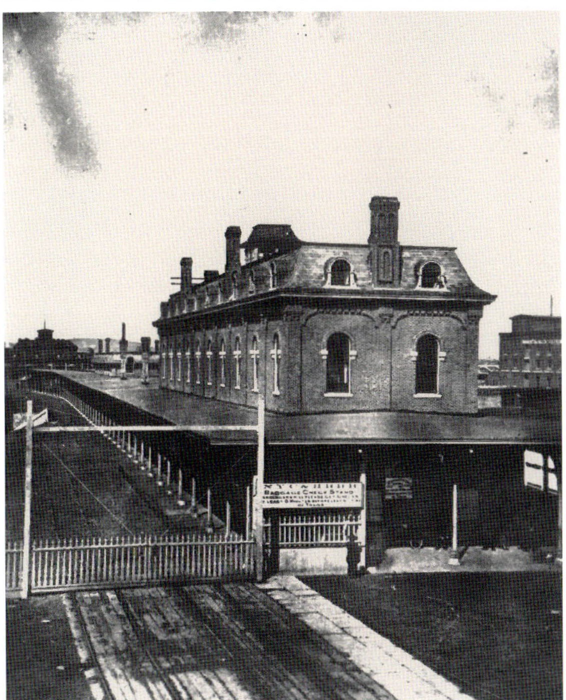

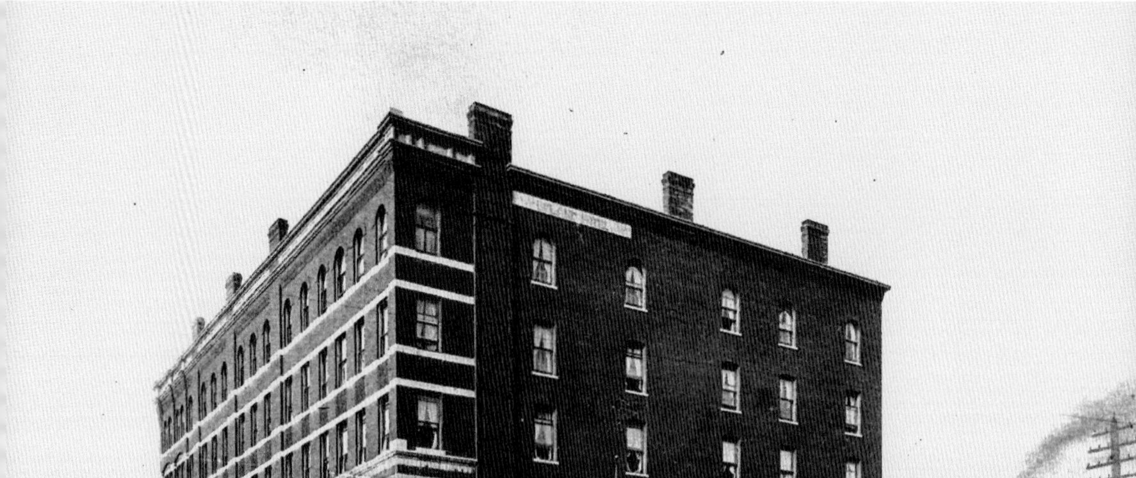

At the time of the second NYCRR station, the Leland Hotel and American Express Company buildings stood just south along South Franklin Street. Constructed in 1888, six stories high with 400 rooms, the Leland Hotel was completely destroyed by one of the worst fires in Syracuse's history in October 1890, taking with it 25 lives. The adjacent American Express Company building also suffered significant damage.

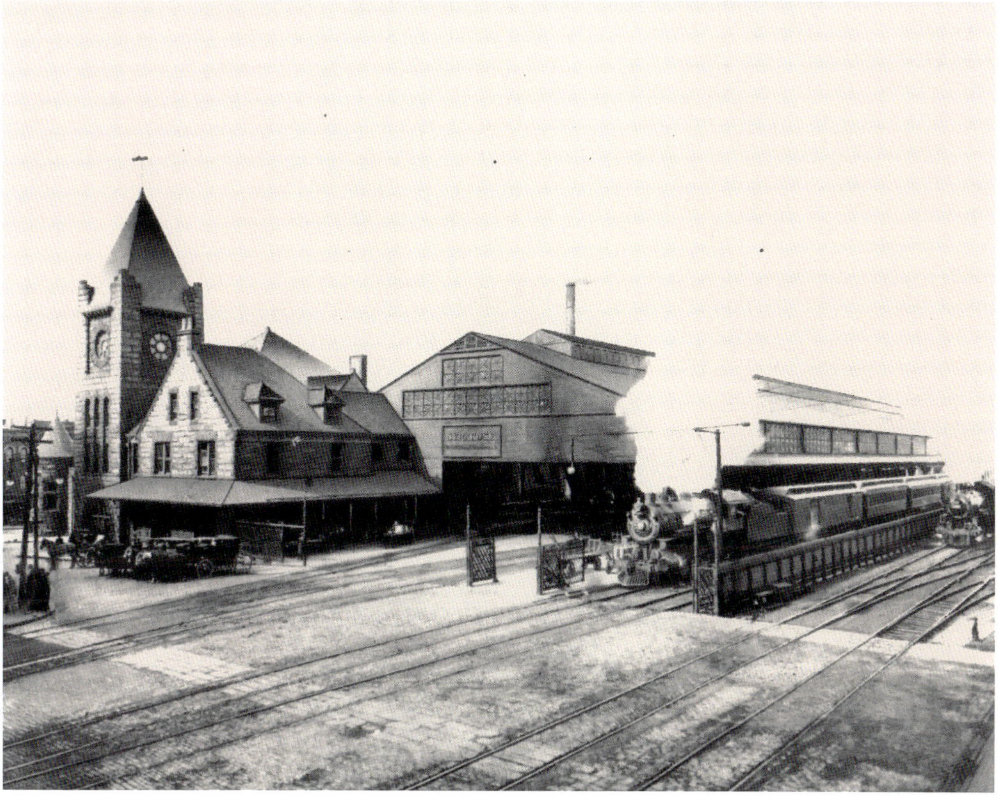

Not long after the rubble was removed in the early 1890s, the third railroad station was constructed in 1896. In 2009, development is planned to begin on a new mixed-use facility offering office, retail, and residential space. (Contemporary image courtesy of QPK Design/ Pioneer Companies.)

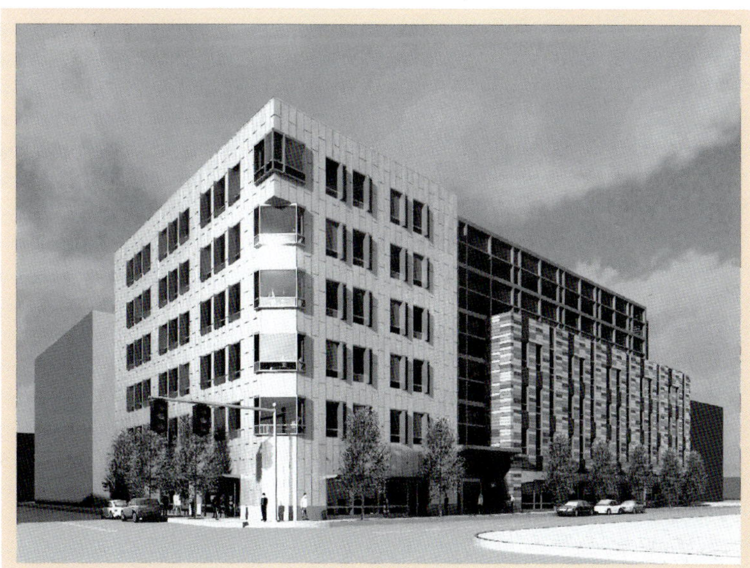

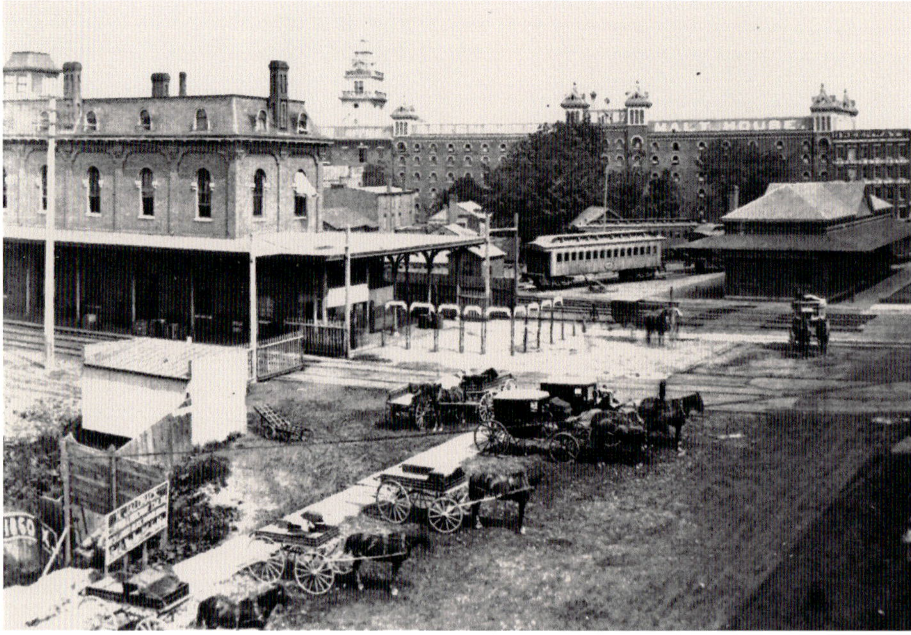

Located north of the NYCRR stations and north of Armory Square, the Greenway Brewery operated in the mid- to late 19th century, becoming the largest Syracuse brewery and largest outside New York City. Brothers George and John Greenway became famous for convincing Syracuse to pipe its water from nearby Lake Skaneateles, still the practice today. While no longer there, another historically significant and magnificent structure stands in its location—the art deco Niagara Mohawk Power Company building, now the offices for National Grid.

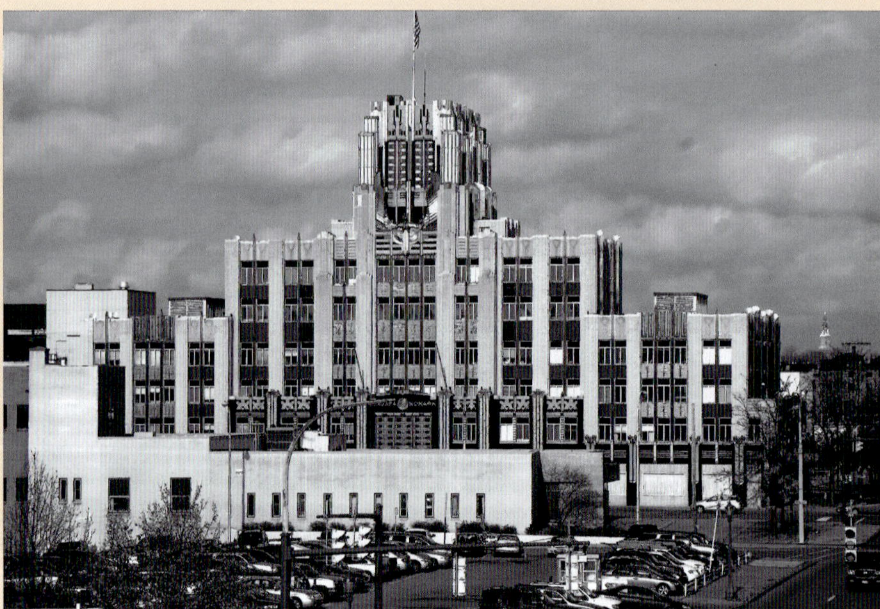

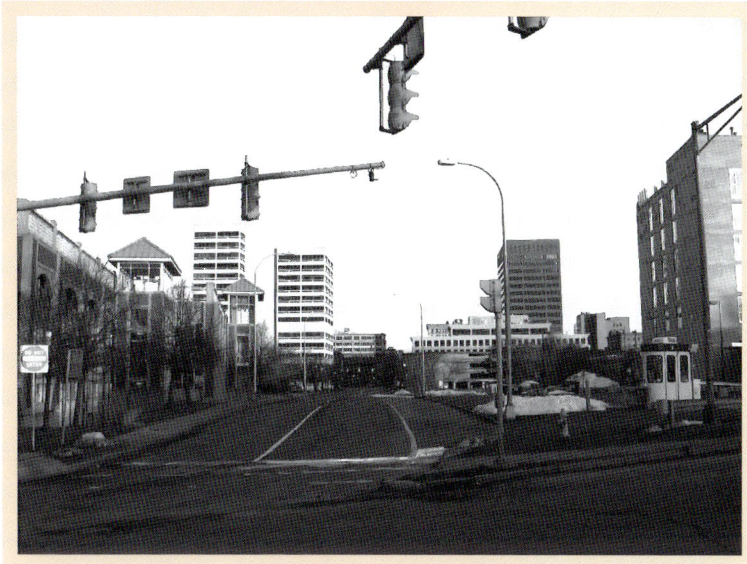

Standing on the west end of West Washington Street looking east, at the intersection with South West Street, a number of buildings have changed. On the right a warehouse still stands but now is used to house teaching facilities for Syracuse University. While on the left the Lehigh Valley Coal Sales company once stood along the railroads connecting to Pennsylvania; now a parking garage stands alongside the roadway, offering covered parking for the many employees at the federal building across the street.

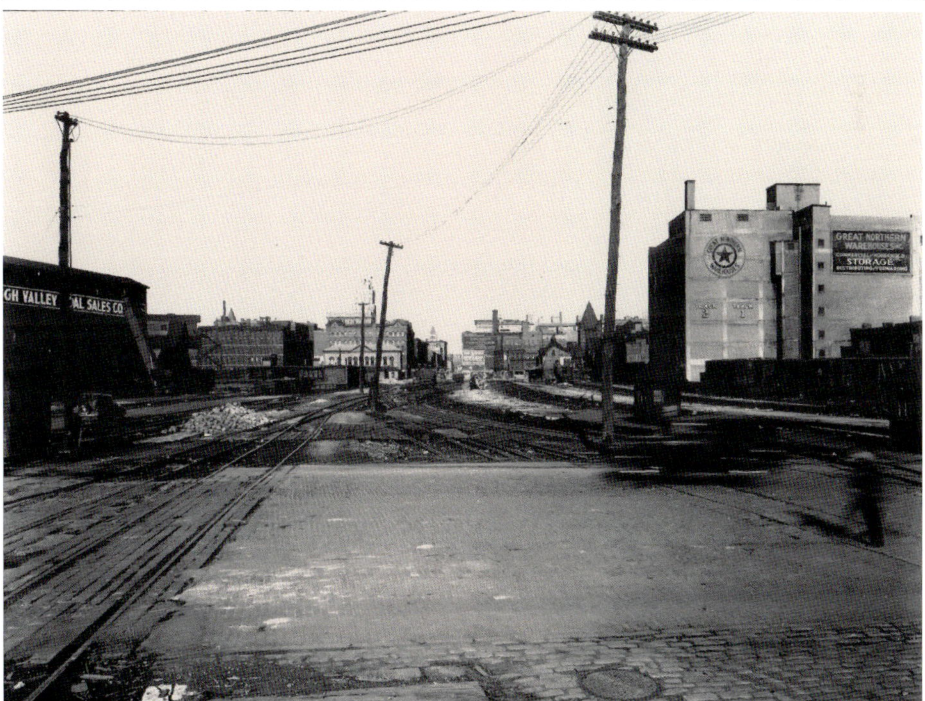

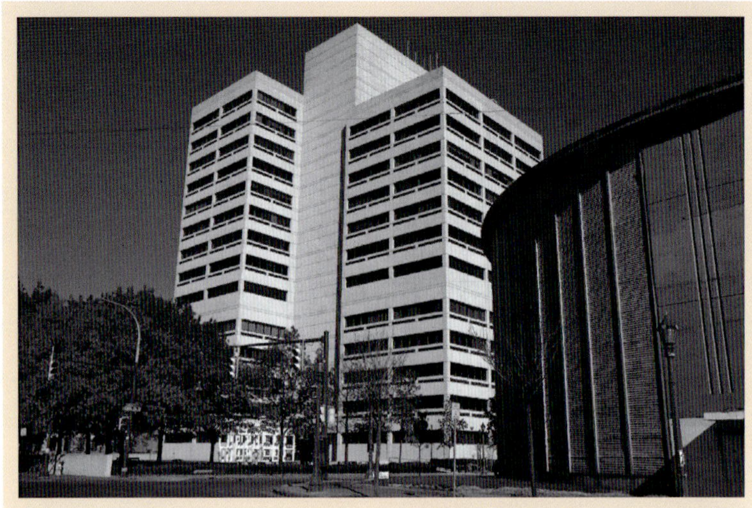

This historic photograph of the northeast corner of South Franklin and West Washington Streets was taken a short time after the construction of the E. W. Edwards Parking Garage in 1956–1957. The rounded corner of the garage can be seen on the right. In the early 1970s, this entire block was demolished and Syracuse's federal building was constructed. Upon his retirement after 16 years in Congress as a representative of the district that included Syracuse, the building was named after United States representative James M. Hanley.

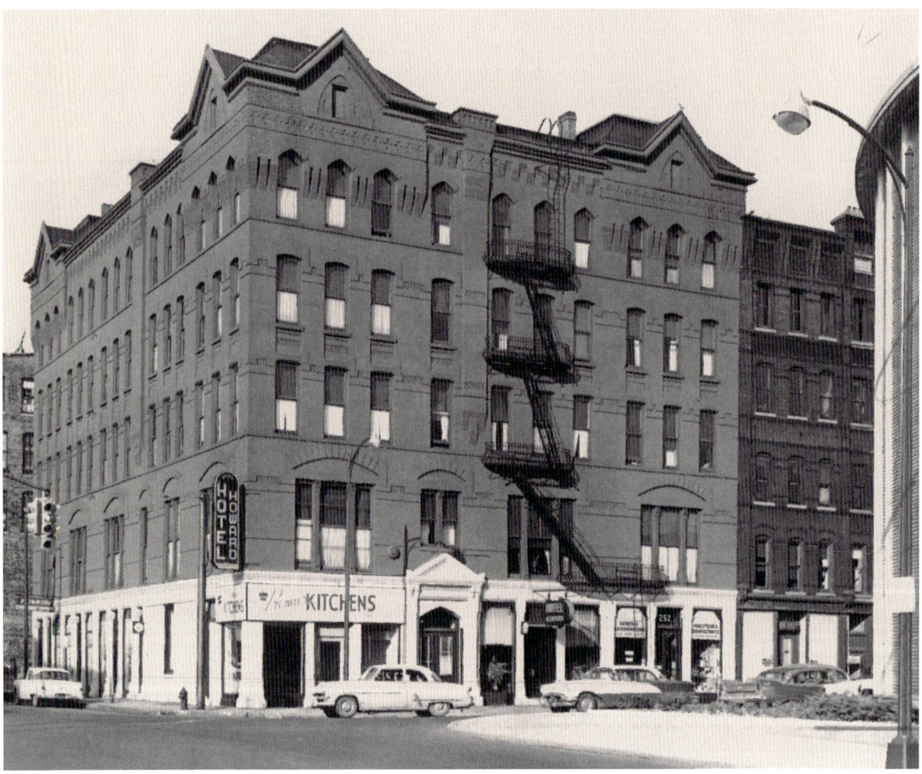

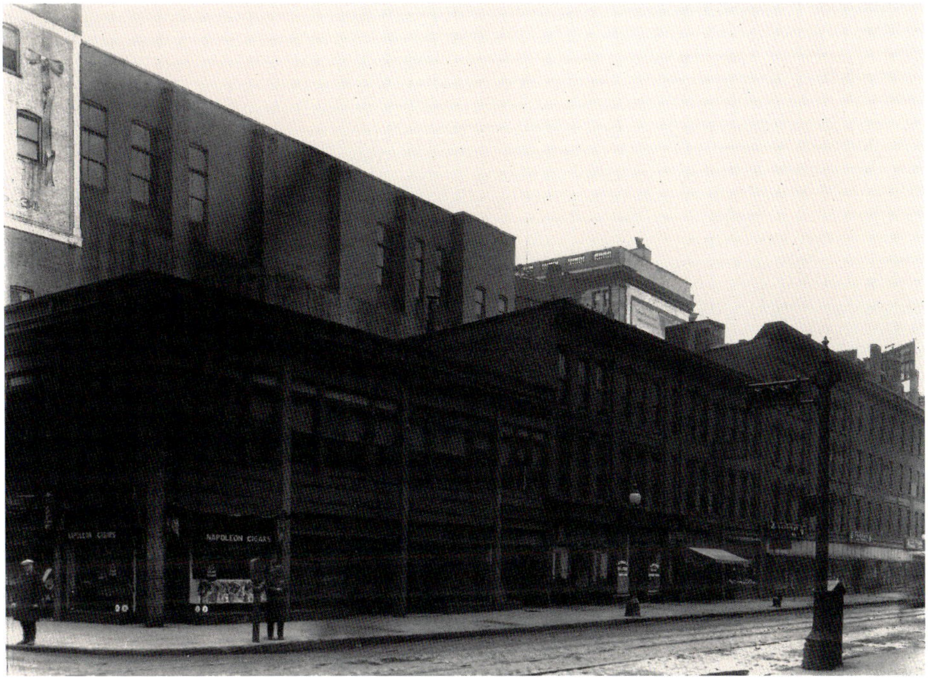

This historic photograph was taken during the period that the NYCRR operated the passenger station a block west. The small two-story building located on the corner of West Washington and South Clinton Streets housed the local offices for the railroad. Today the Atrium Building is located on this block adjacent to Clinton Square. The facility provides office space for several businesses, and in 2008, the State University of New York at Oswego opened the Metro Center here, offering a variety of courses.

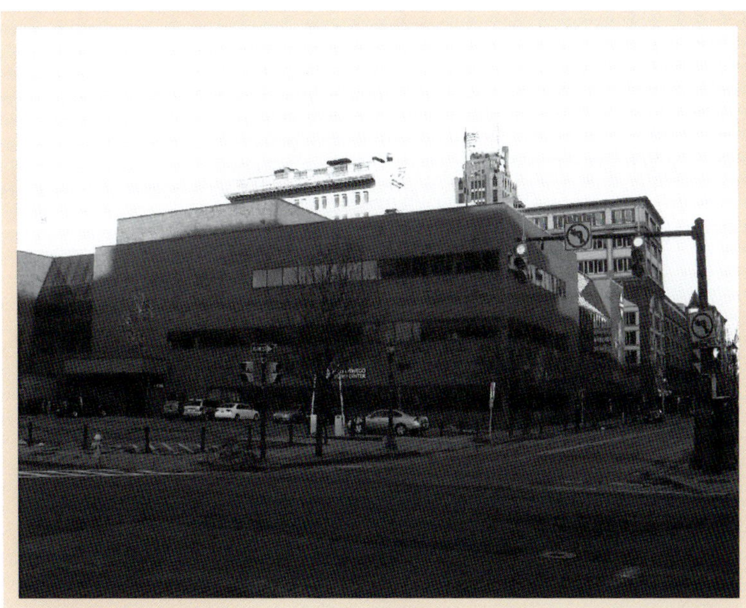

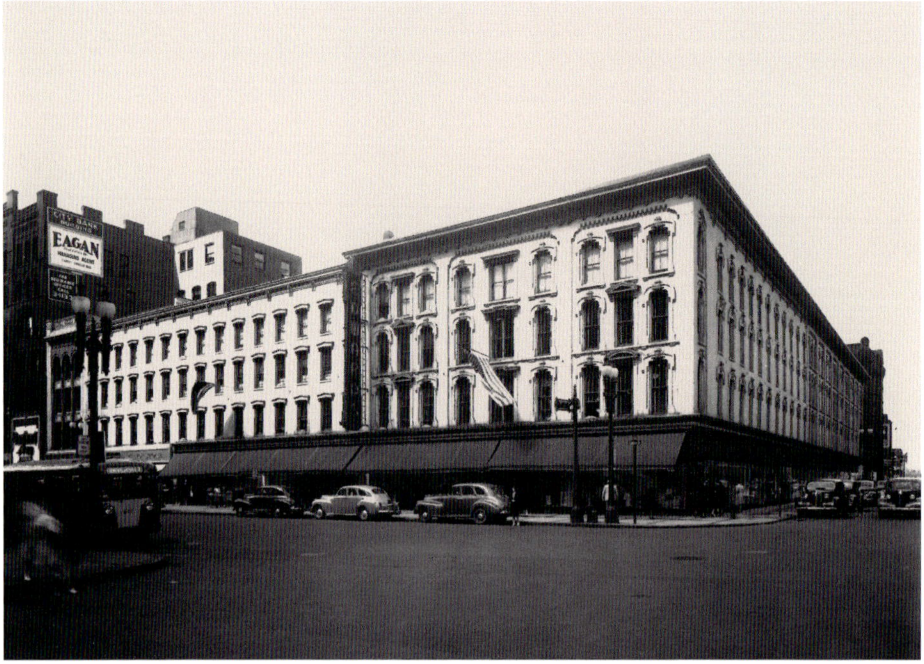

By 1970, one of the largest of several downtown Syracuse clothing and department stores was E. W. Edwards, located at the corner of West Washington and South Salina Streets. In 1972, it moved to a new building on the side of Clinton Square, which was the first phase of a larger urban renewal project. When Edwards moved, its original building was demolished to make way for the second phase of the project, the construction of the Lincoln Tower. The third phase was not completed, and it remains a surface parking lot between the tower and West Washington Street.

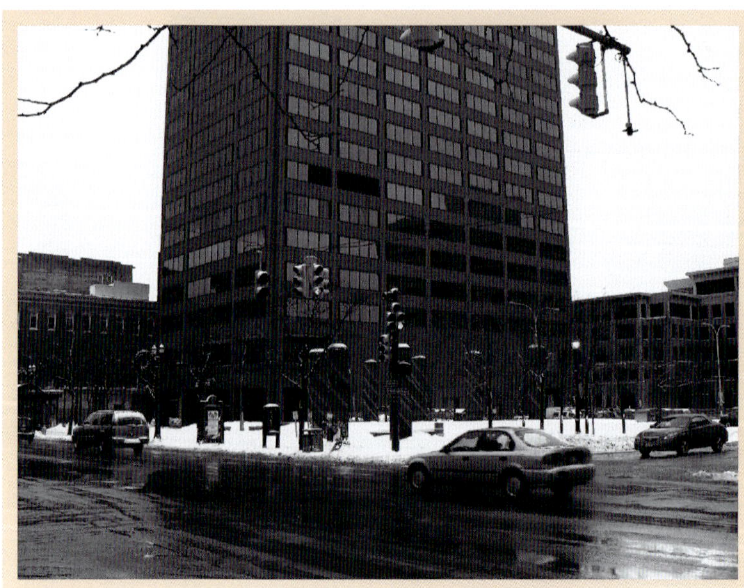

CHAPTER 4

West Fayette Street

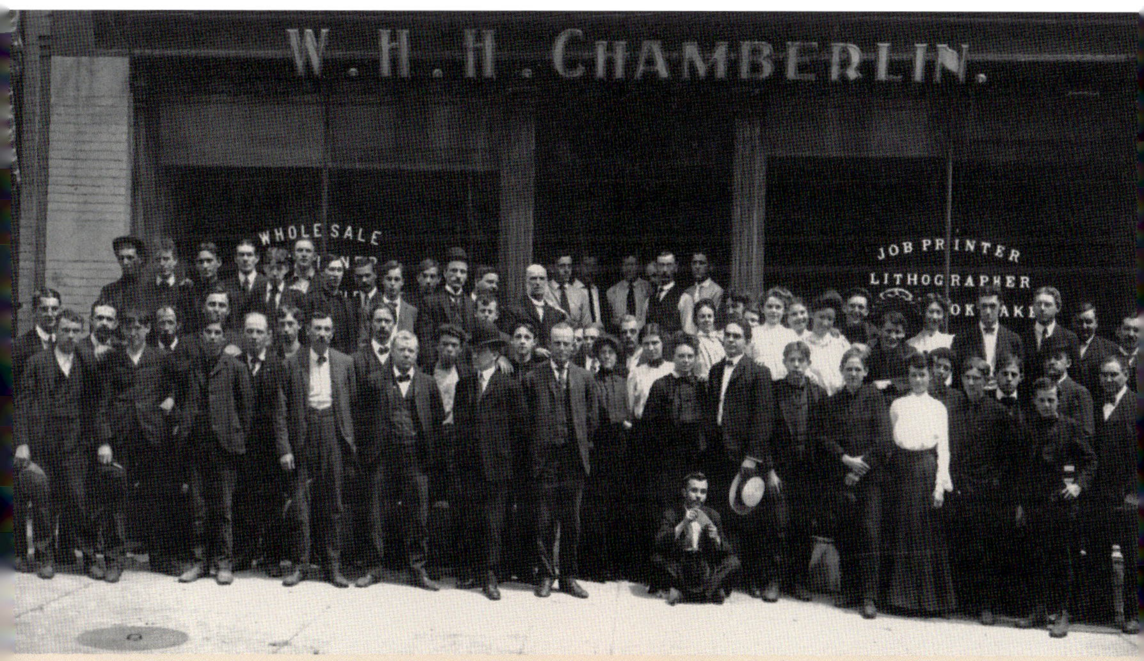

This undated photograph was taken outside W. H. H. Chamberlin, Inc., which first opened in 1895. The company was located in two locations on West Fayette Street. Both buildings still exist today, and this one featured was bought by W. H. H. Chamberlin in the 1930s and today still bears his name. As can be seen from the writing on the storefront windows, Chamberlin's was a stationer.

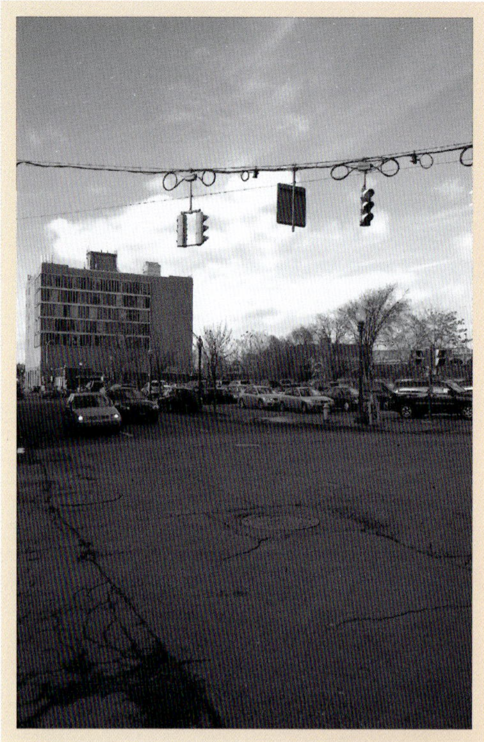

The historic photograph featured is another look at the old NYCRR passenger station on West Fayette Street at the corner of South Franklin Street. This view is looking west where today there is a parking lot, although development will begin soon on two hotels on this site. The Syracuse University Warehouse building can be seen in the distance of the contemporary photograph.

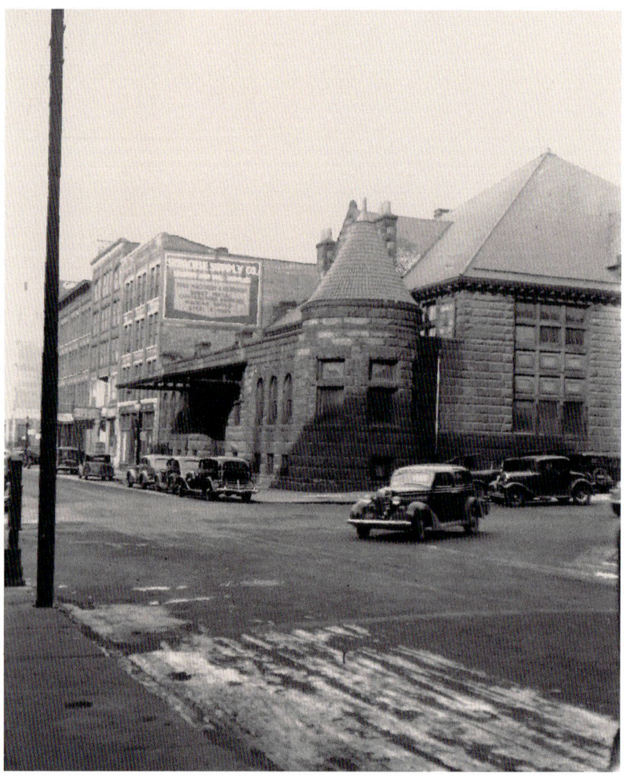

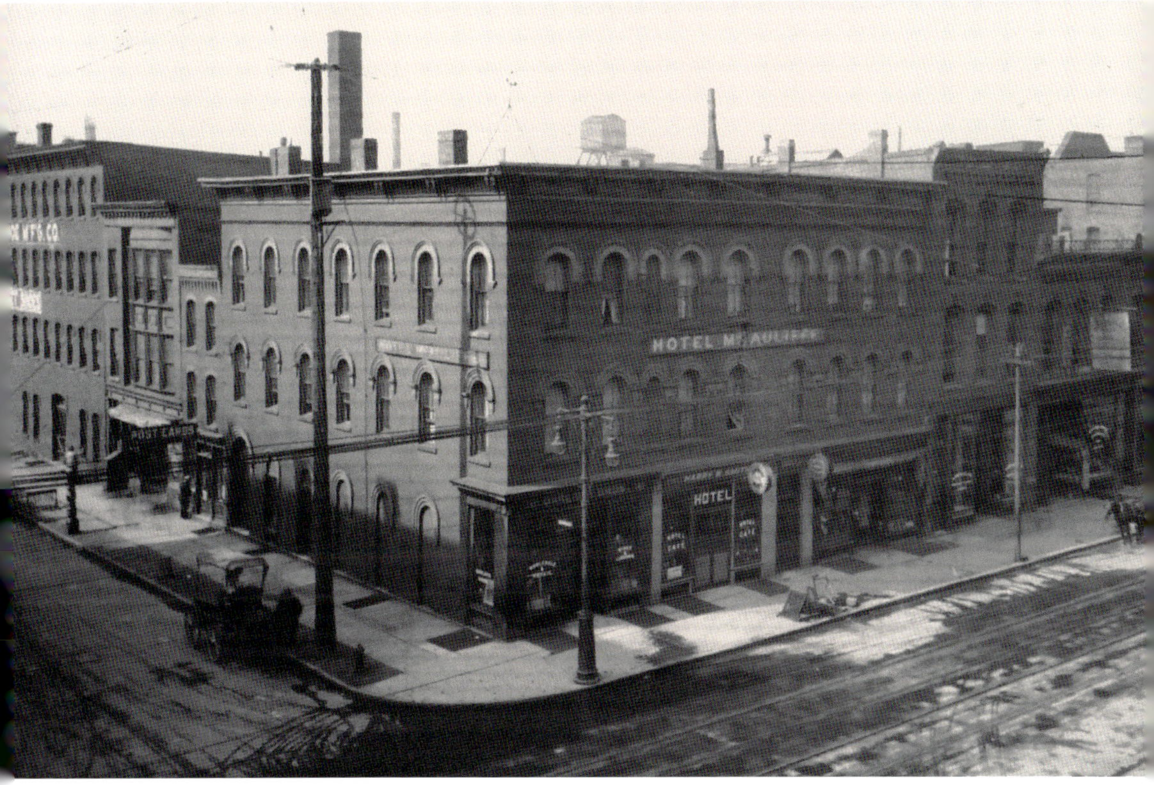

While the building pictured in this historic image bears the name Hotel McAuliffe, it is actually the very well-known Crown Hotel building. Originally built in 1876 when the railroad industry—and subsequently this neighborhood—began to boom, this hotel was located right across the street from the NYCRR station. The building was renovated in the 1990s and became the Crown Bar and Grill. Today the popular Kitty Hoyne's Irish Pub calls the Crown home. Office space is on the upper floors.

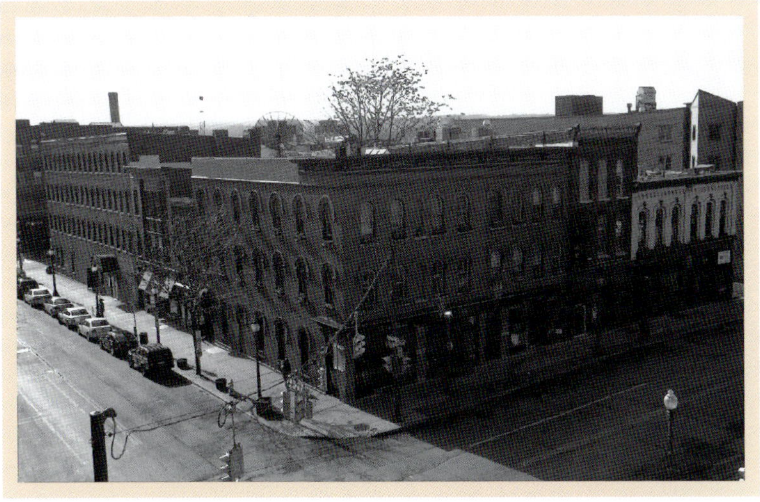

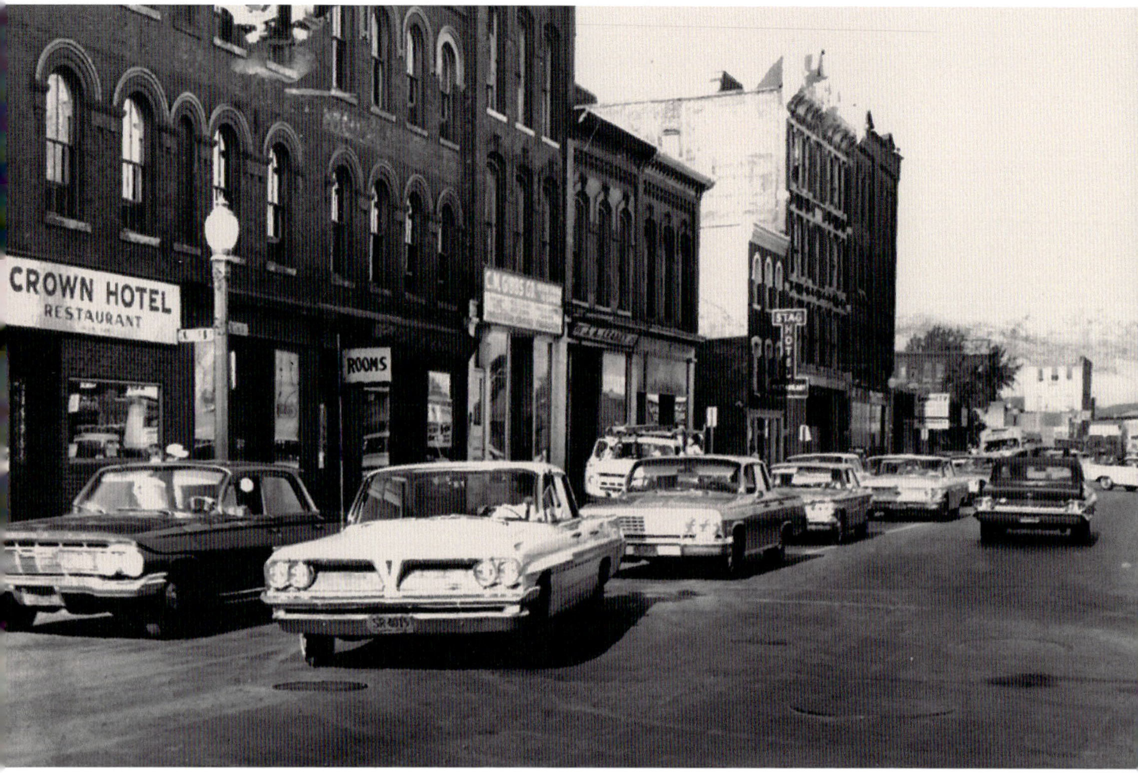

Going from aerial to street level, the Crown Hotel sign can be seen in this terrific photograph looking west down Fayette Street from the South Franklin Street corner. Next to the Crown Hotel was the C. M. Gibb's Company (built in the 1870s), with the Stag Hotel and Mill Pond Landing Building to the west. Gibb's was a canvas store manufacturing awnings and other products. Most of these buildings remain today on this block, although a few are vacant and for sale.

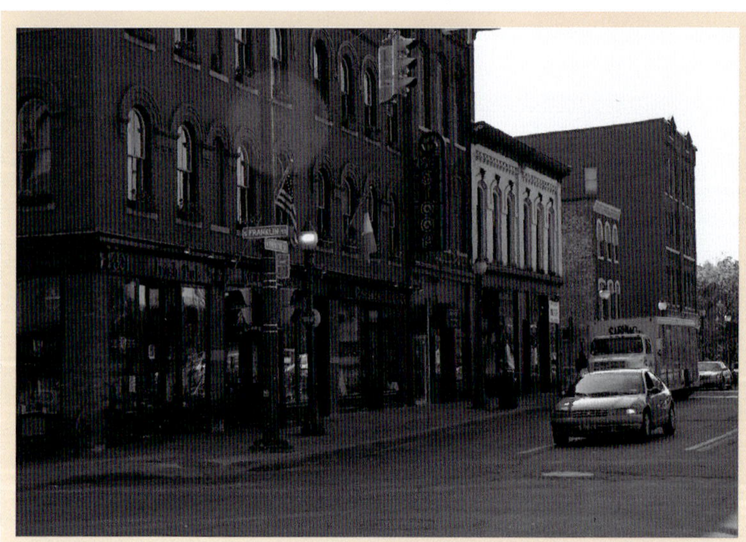

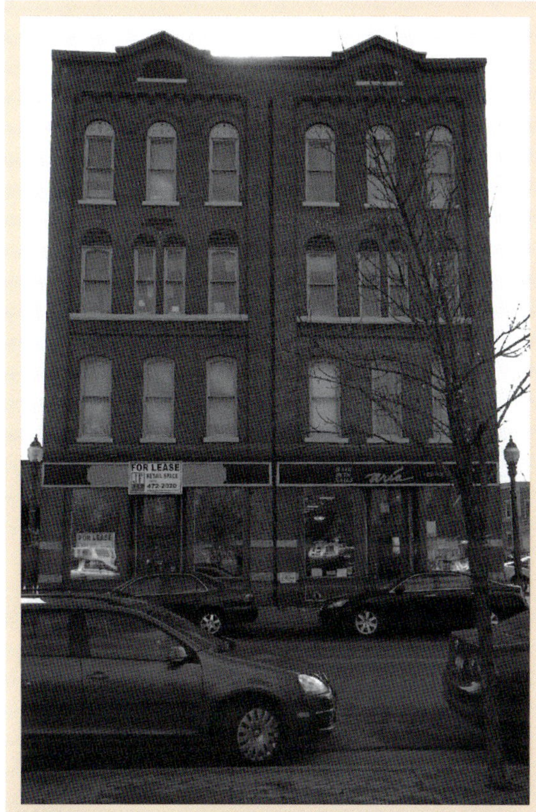

This more recent historic photograph was taken in 1979, prior to the extensive renovation of the historically significant Mill Pond Landing Building. Originally a three-story building constructed in 1878 for wholesale grocer A. S. Coan and Company, a fourth story was added in 1896. A group of investors completed renovating the building in 1989 so that it could provide modern retail and office space. (Historic image courtesy of George W. Curry.)

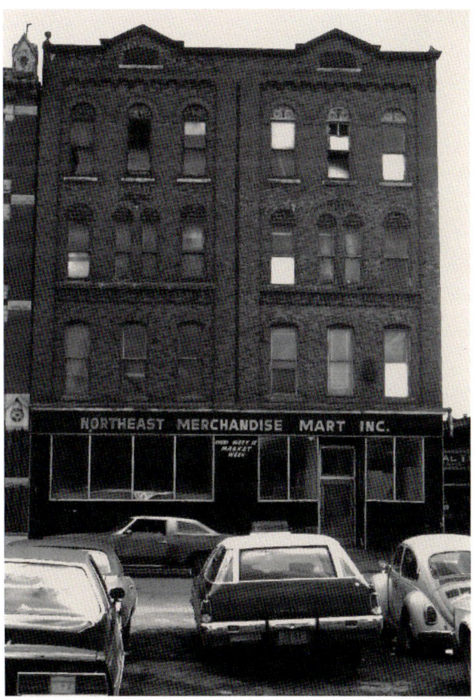

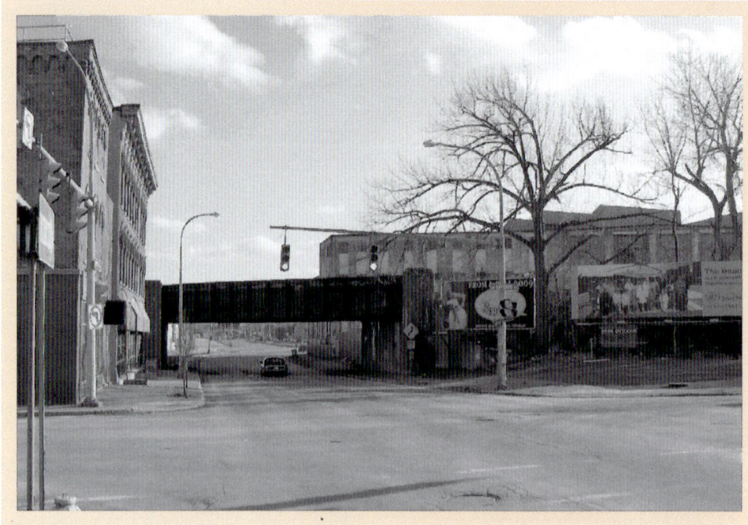

The streetscape has changed drastically from the time of this original photograph looking south down South West Street, at the intersection of West Fayette Street. A railroad crossing sign and DL&W train cars can be seen on the right. While those same railroad tracks remain across the street today, the track was elevated in 1936 to accommodate automobile traffic. Today the Redhouse theater is located in the first building on the left.

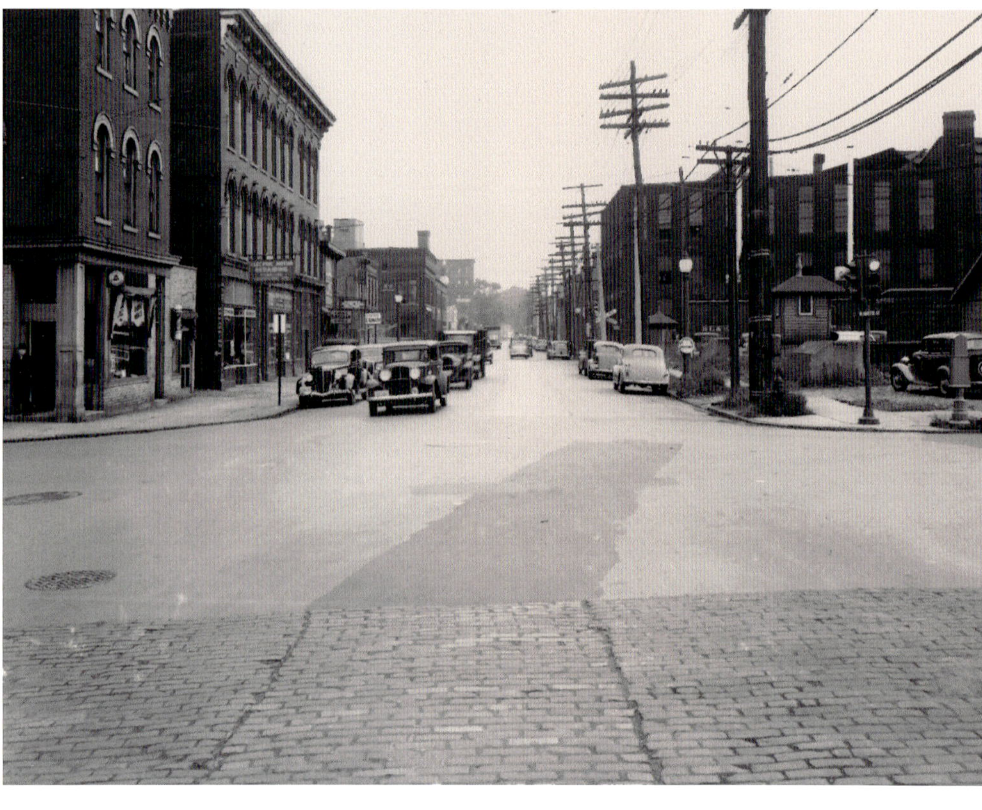

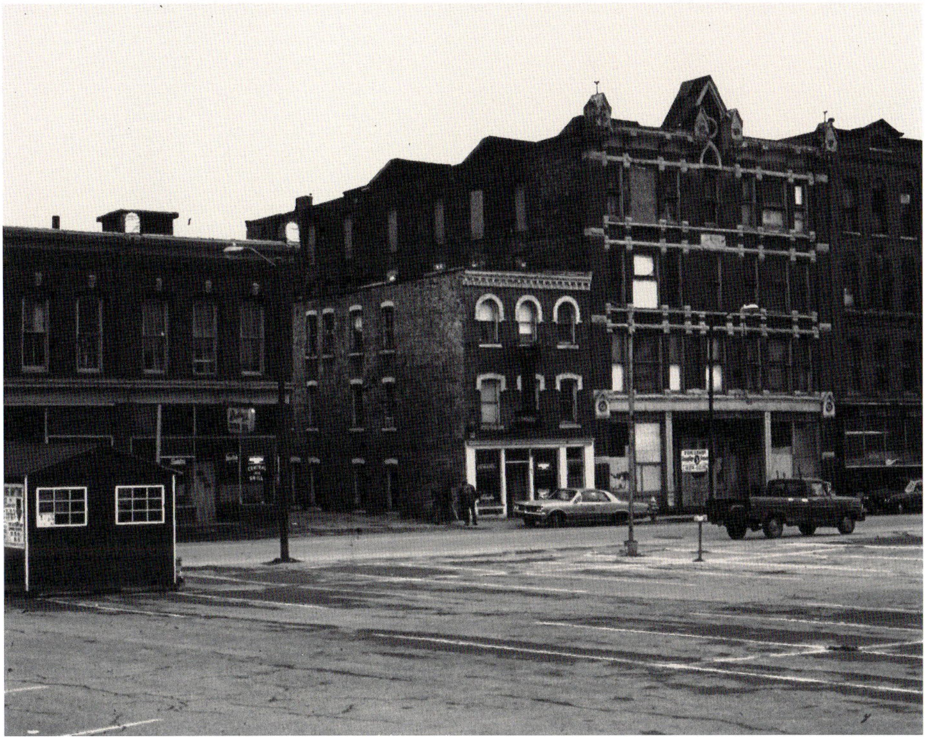

In this photograph showing the buildings just west of the Crown Hotel, the Stag Hotel can be seen in the center. This hotel was originally built in the 1870s as the City Hotel, and as of early 2009, it remains open, making it the longest-standing hotel in the Armory Square district. (Historic image courtesy of George W. Curry.)

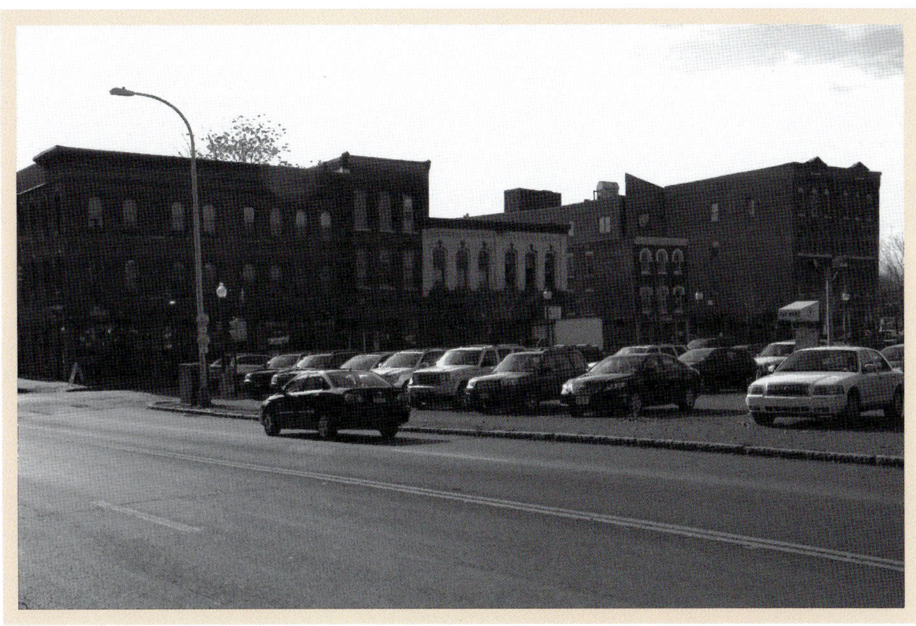

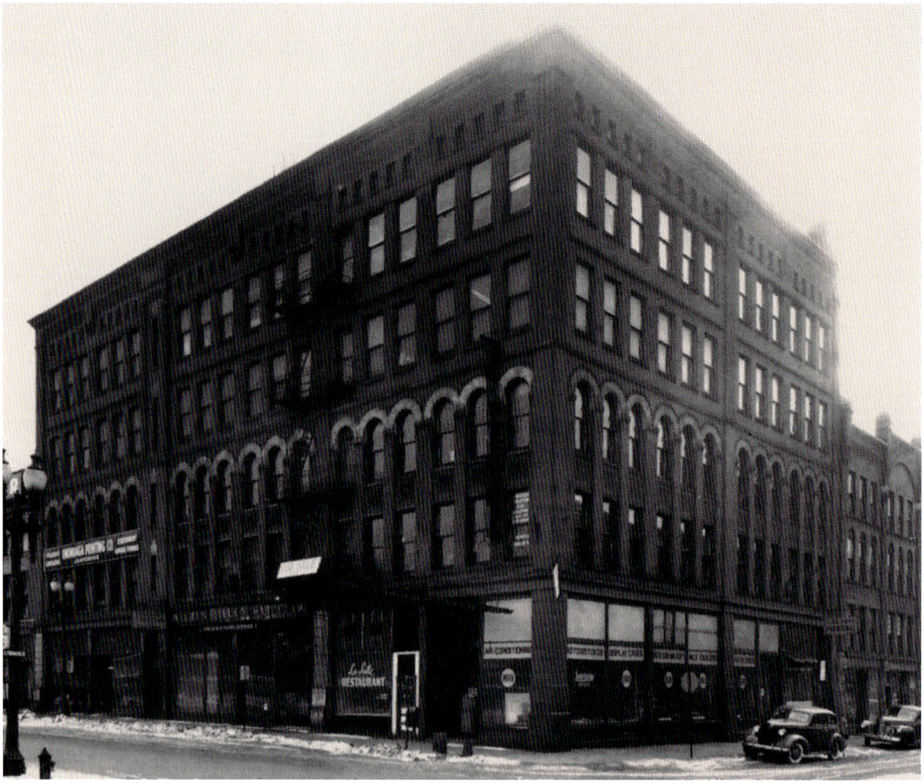

Less than a year after the tragic Leland Hotel fire in 1890 that claimed 25 lives and destroyed the hotel on the northwest corner of West Fayette and South Franklin Streets, another large fire destroyed the buildings across the street in March 1891. Attorney Thomas Hogan, in 1895, constructed the Hogan Block at this southeast corner. Renovations from 1985 to 1987 created new space for retail, restaurants, offices, and residential apartments in this large structure.

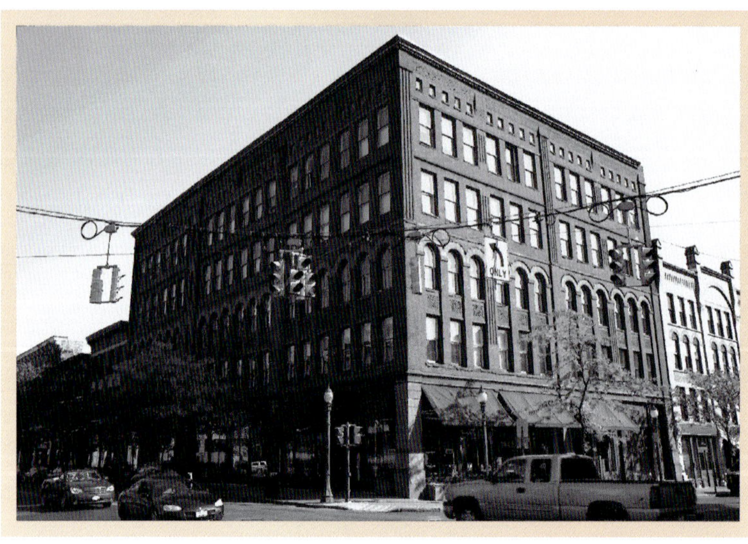

While Seubert and Warner, manufacturers and retailers of cigars, originally owned this building when it was built in 1875, the Garret Paper Company operated here for a long period of time. The first edition of the *Syracuse Herald* newspaper was printed in this building on January 14, 1877. Today it is connected to the structure to the right and the combined facility is known as the Seneca Building, offering retail and restaurant/bar space below with office space above.

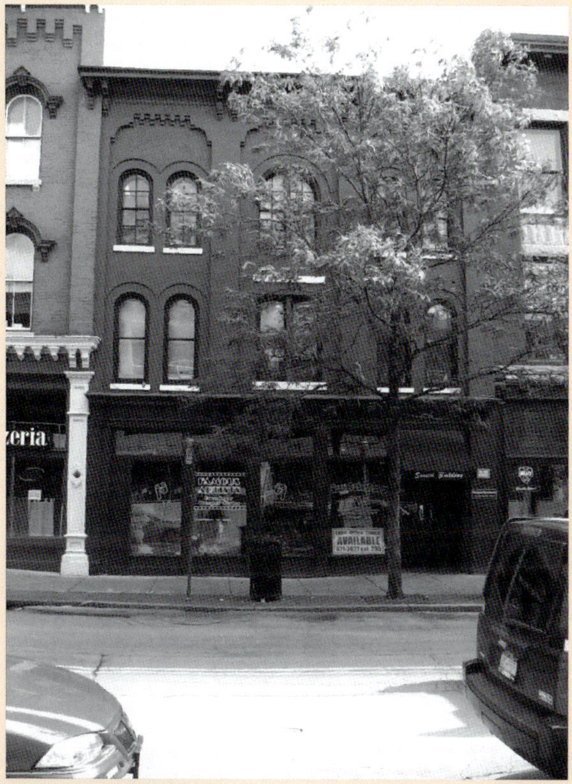

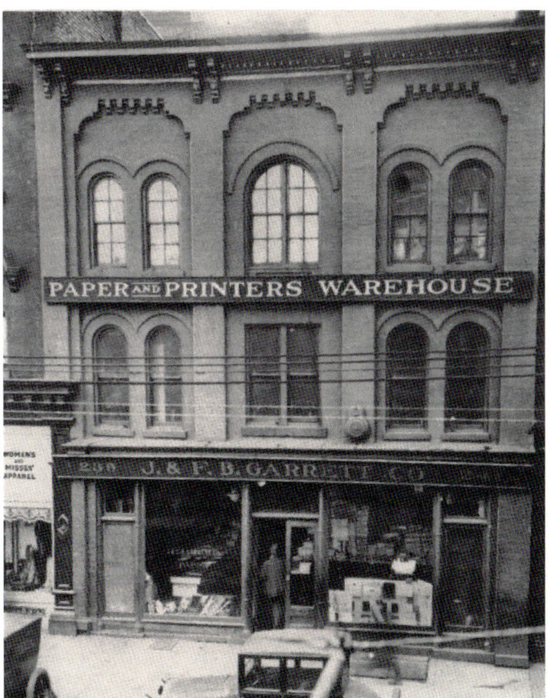

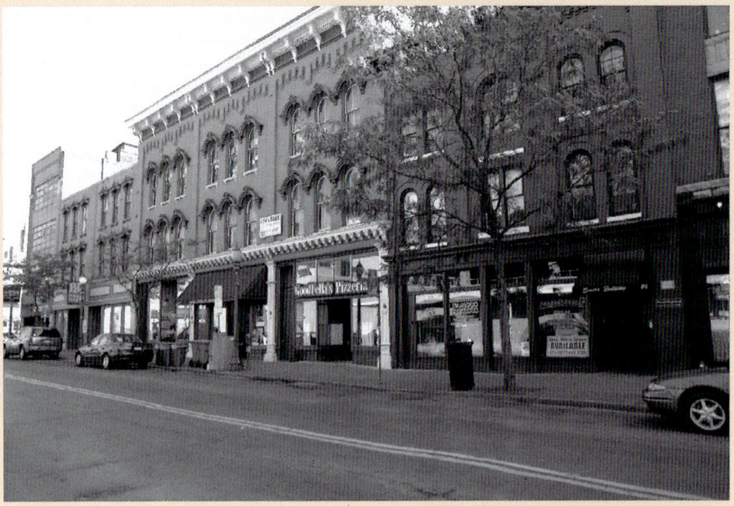

Adjacent to the Seneca Building, the Piper-Phillips Block was constructed around 1872. Originally the space was used for retail below with residential hotel rooms above for railroad employees. As with much of the space in Armory Square, after the railroads left the area, the space was left vacant. This historic photograph was taken in 1976, prior to the extensive renovations in 1987. Today the block provides retail and office space and is connected with the Bentley-Settle Building behind on Walton Street. (Historic image courtesy of George W. Curry.)

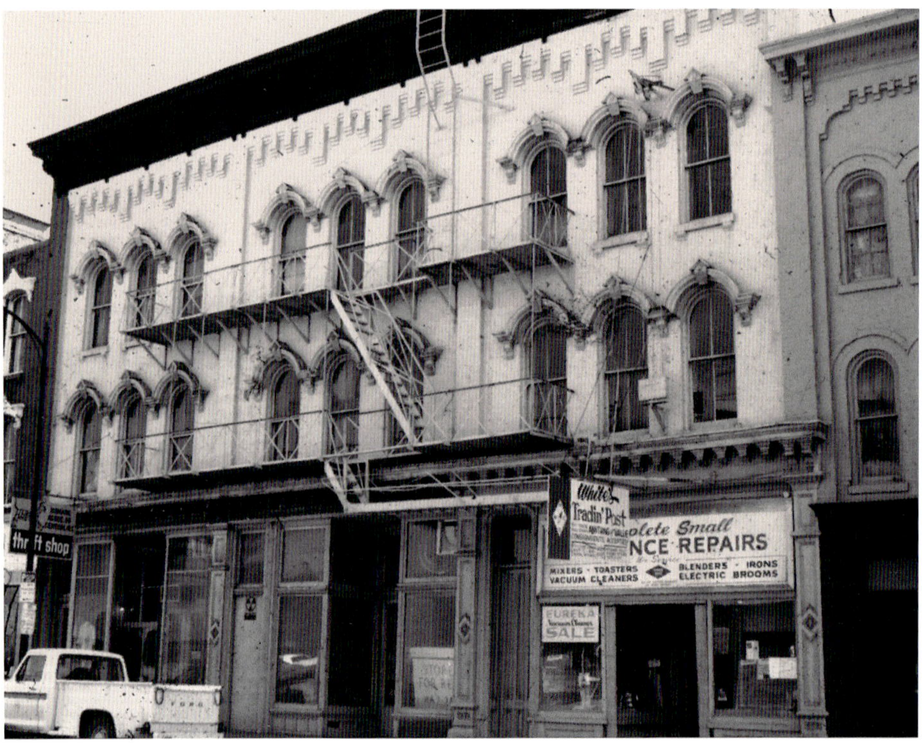

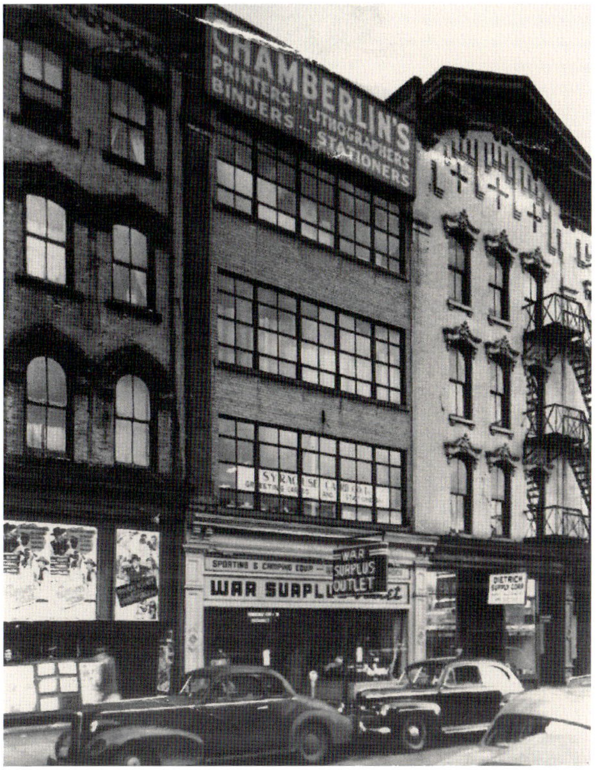

While not immediately evident, the structures pictured in this pair of photographs are actually the same. The demolished St. Cloud Hotel once stood to the left of the Chamberlin building, which was once known as the Tallman Block.

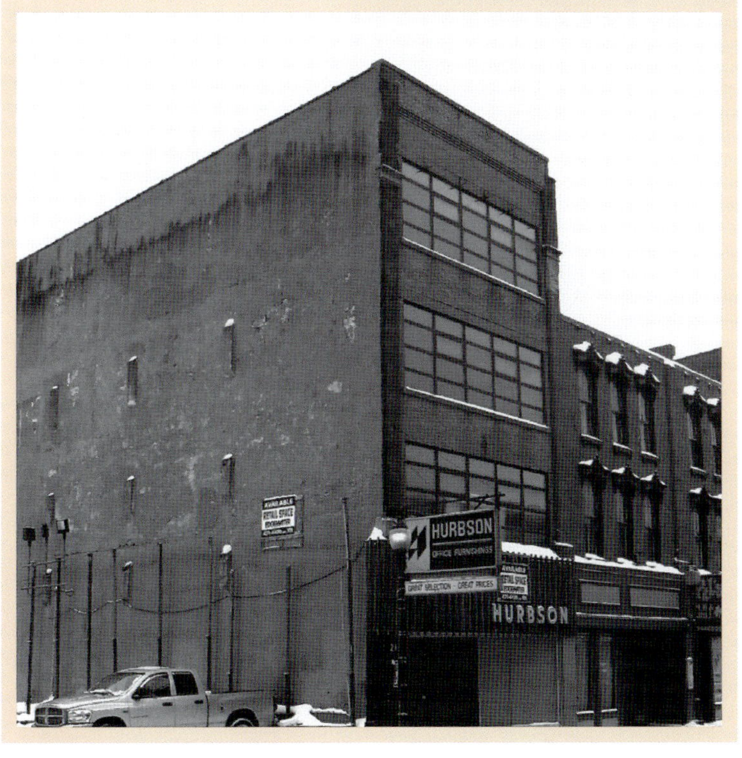

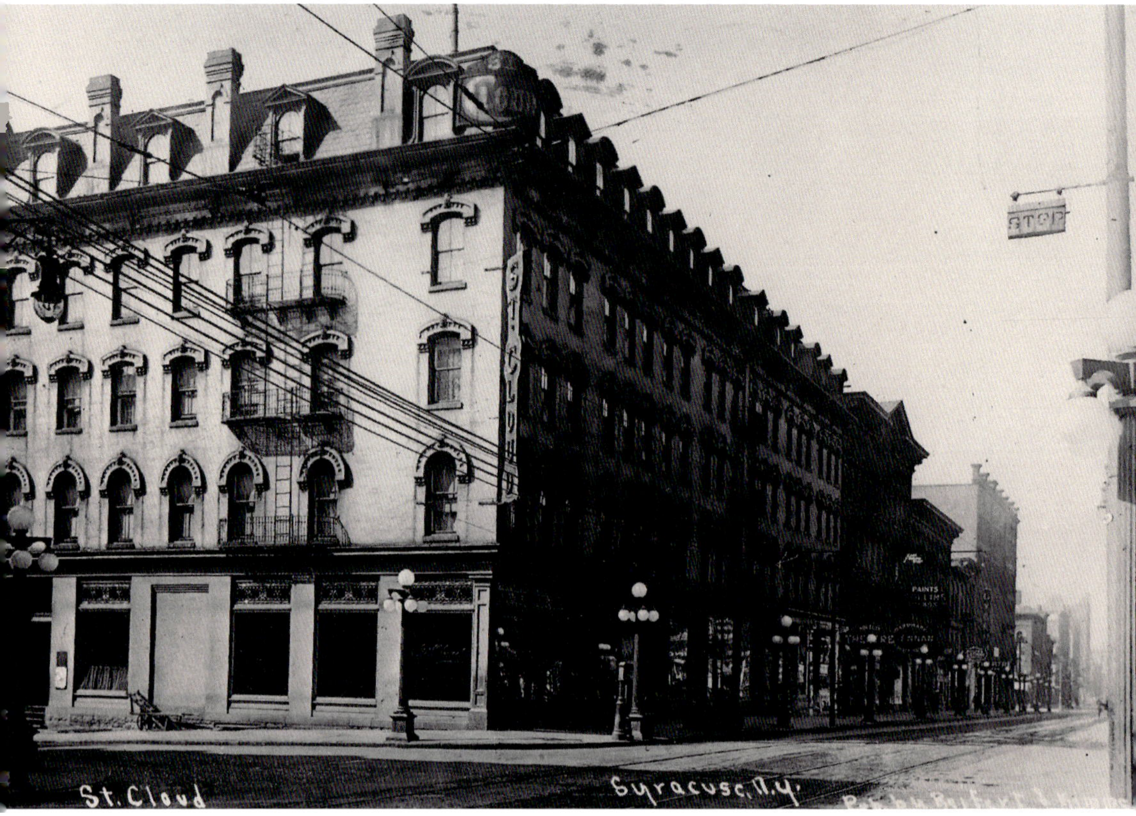

The hotel pictured here underwent many name changes throughout the years. Built in 1870, it was at one time known as the Hotel Burns, later renamed the better-known St. Cloud Hotel in 1897. With the relocation of the railroad stations outside downtown Syracuse in the 1930s, the building would later be demolished in 1953 to make way for a parking lot.

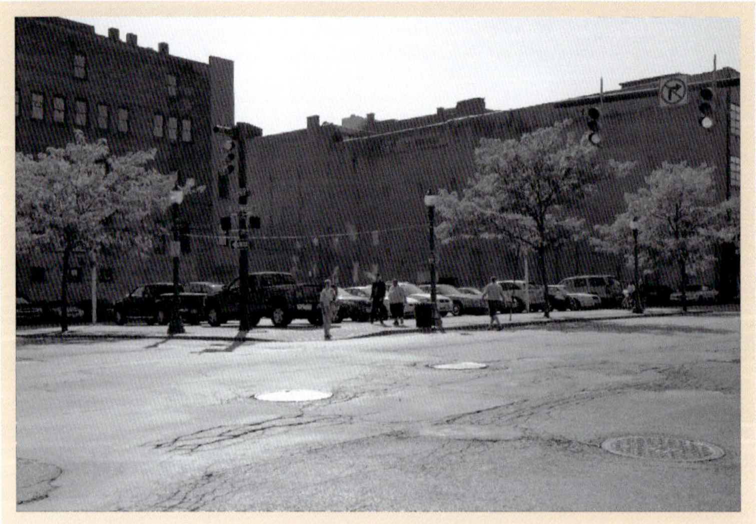

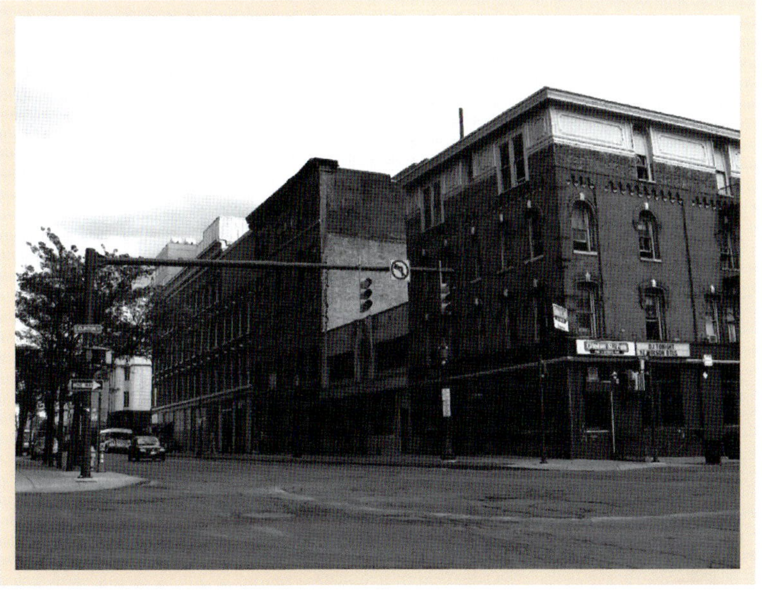

Across the street, on the southeast corner of West Fayette and South Clinton Streets, the Kirk Hotel is located. This and other nearby buildings were owned at one time by William Kirk, a wagon maker who later became one of the wealthiest men in Syracuse after investing in railroad stock. This hotel, built around 1870, has undergone many changes and will soon be redeveloped significantly to help meet the demand for more residential space in Armory Square.

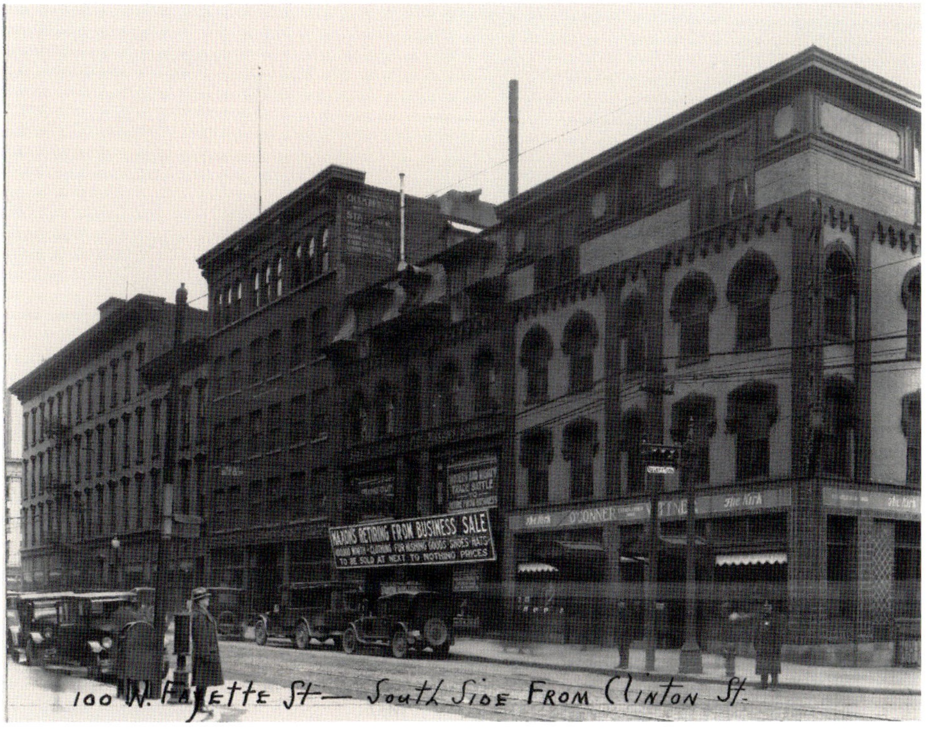

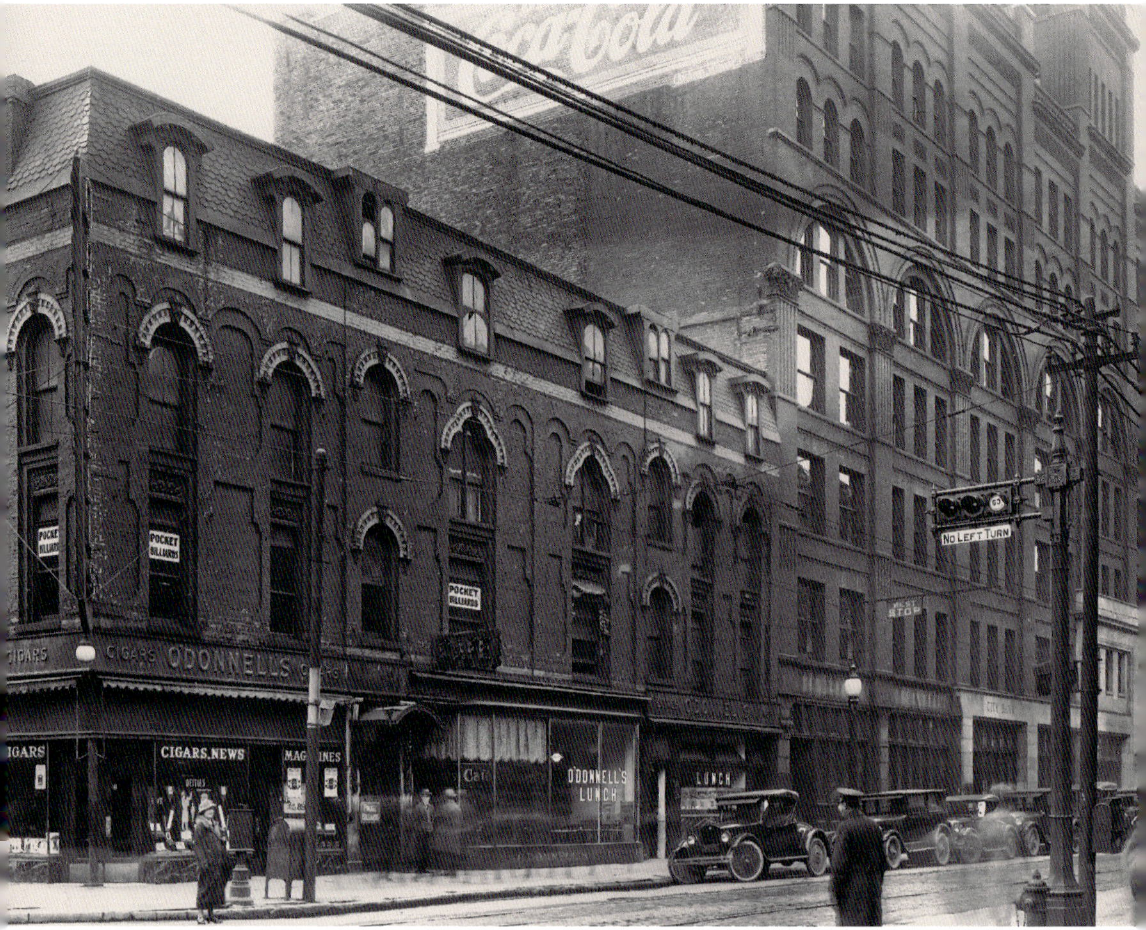

In 1869, the Andrews Building was constructed on the northeast corner of West Fayette and South Clinton Streets. A cigar and newspaper store operated in this location during the time of this photograph.

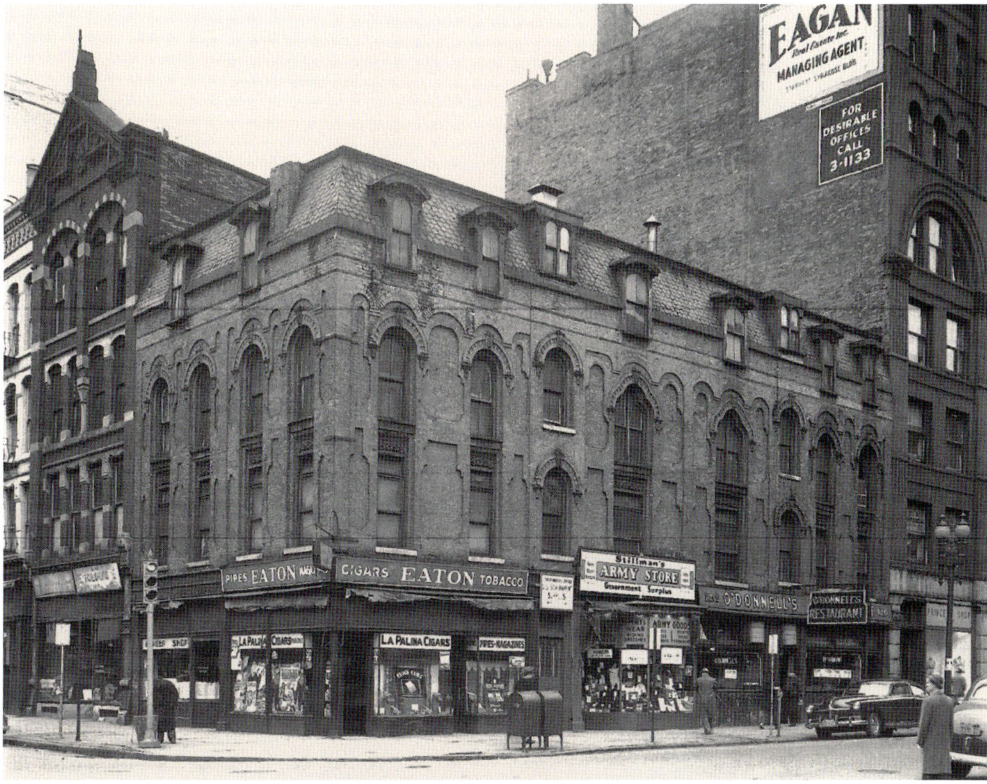

In this later photograph of the Andrews Building taken in 1939, the cigar store remains and a new store sign can be seen for an army surplus store—one of two that can be seen in historic photographs from this neighborhood. The building was demolished in 1970, and soon after One Lincoln Center was built on this block.

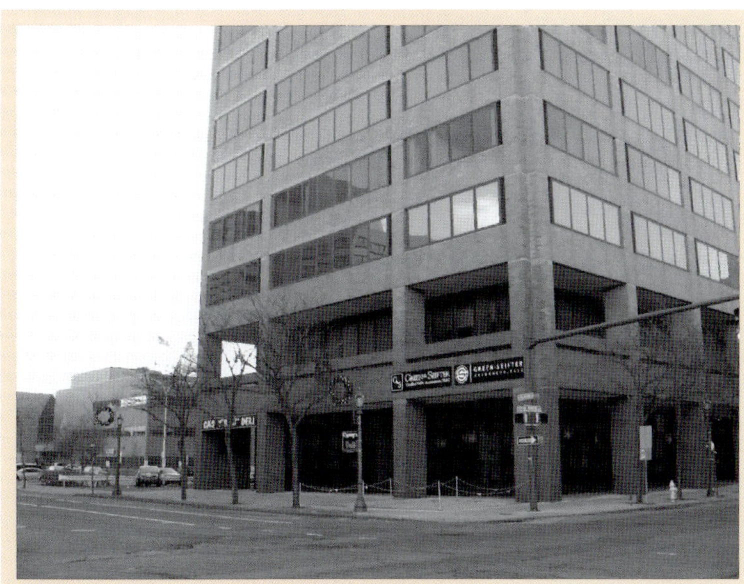

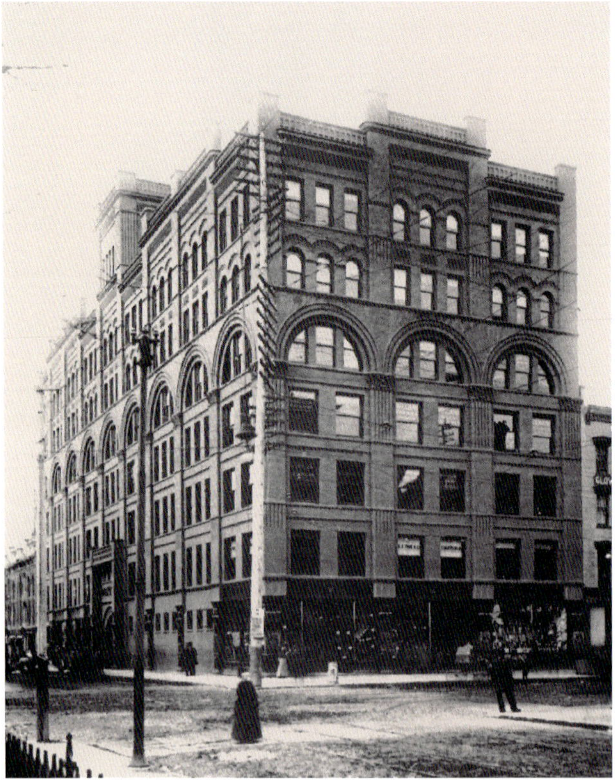

William Kirk's son, William B. Kirk, also an accomplished businessman as well as former mayor of Syracuse, built what was then known as the Kirk Fireproof Building in 1897. Located just east of the Andrews Building on the corner of West Fayette and South Salina Streets, the building later became better known as the City Bank Building, until it was demolished in 1970 to make way for the 19-story Lincoln building.

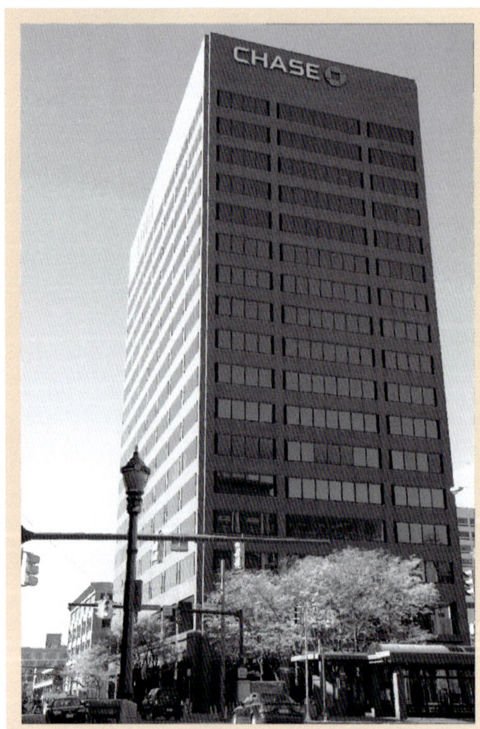

CHAPTER 5

South Salina Street

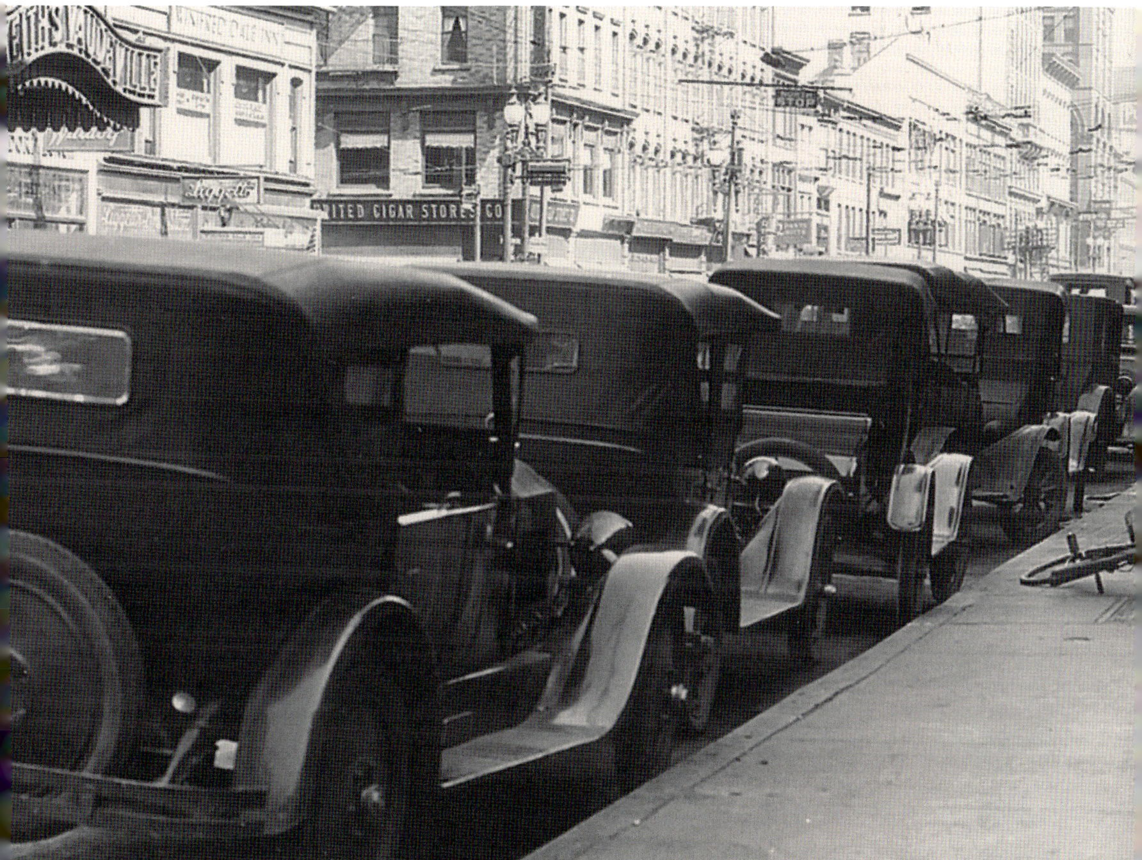

South Salina Street has always been the main street for downtown Syracuse. The historic core was the 300 block. Architecturally it contains many of the city's most significant commercial buildings and was listed in the National Register of Historic Places in 2009. During the 1960s, the population shifted to the suburbs and Salina Street began to decline. However, the future is bright. Many rehabilitation projects are planned.

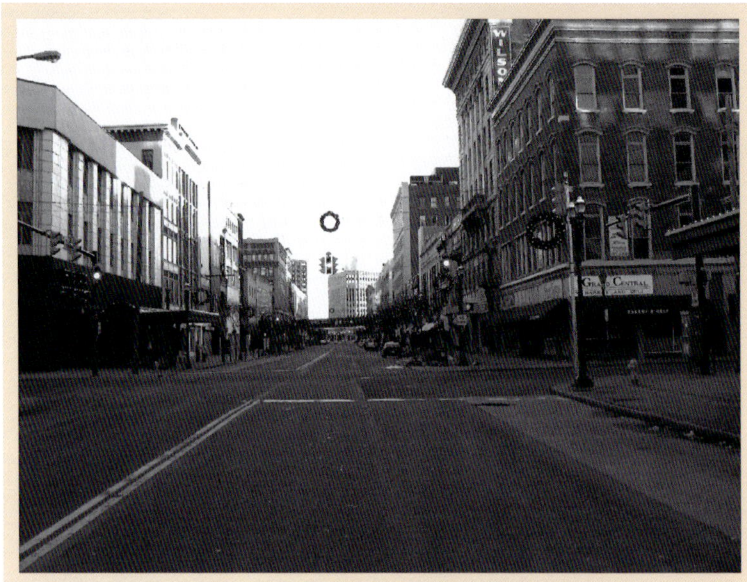

Seen here is the 300 block of South Salina Street looking south from the intersection of Fayette Street. In the *c.* 1940 photograph, the block is filled with clothing, shoe, stationery, drug, and department stores and theaters, most notably Dey Brothers on the right and Witherill's on the left. Upper floors were filled with offices. In 2009, it is quite different. Most buildings are empty on the upper floors, and only a handful of retailers are on the street level.

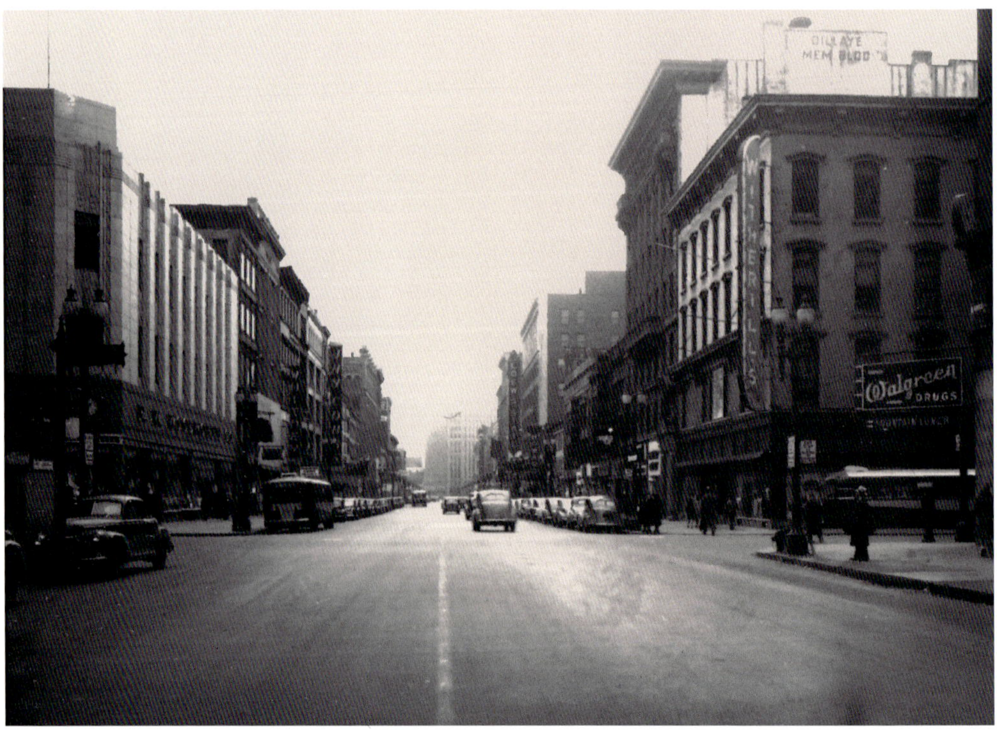

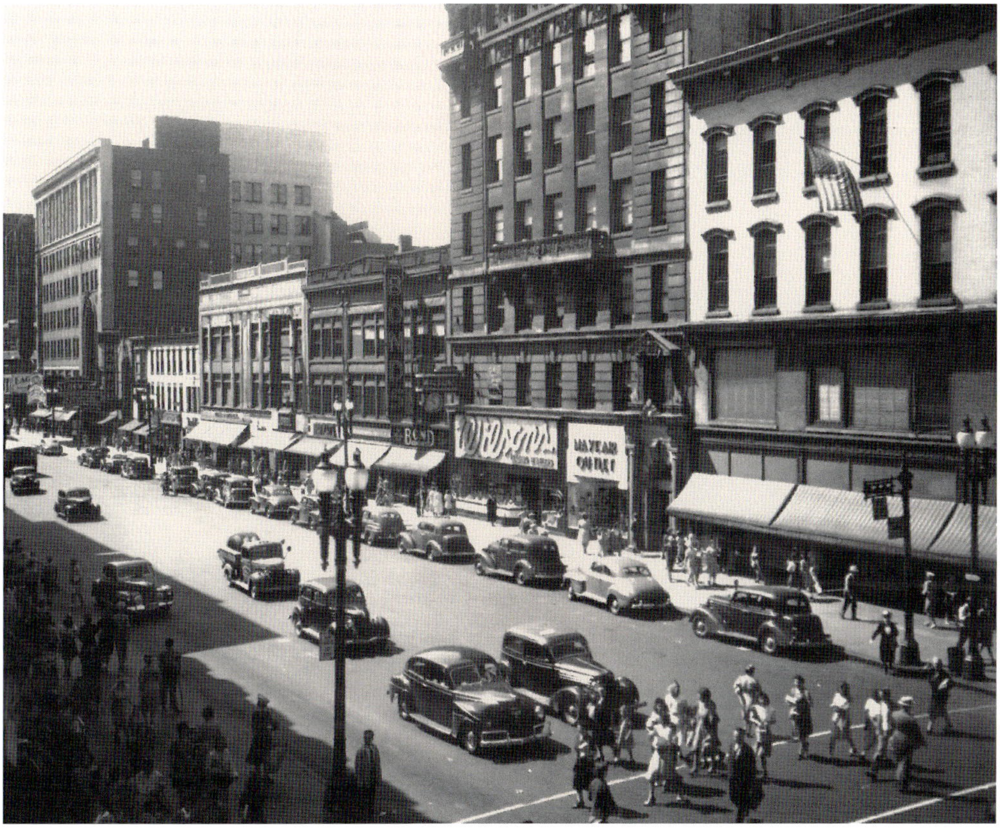

Shoppers fill the sidewalks of the 300 block of South Salina Street in this 1944 photograph. The Loew's State Theater was showing *The Seventh Cross* and *One Mysterious Night*. With many storefronts and upper-floor offices vacant, shoppers are no longer filling the sidewalks. With the 2009 national historic district designation, many of these buildings will become attractive to local developers.

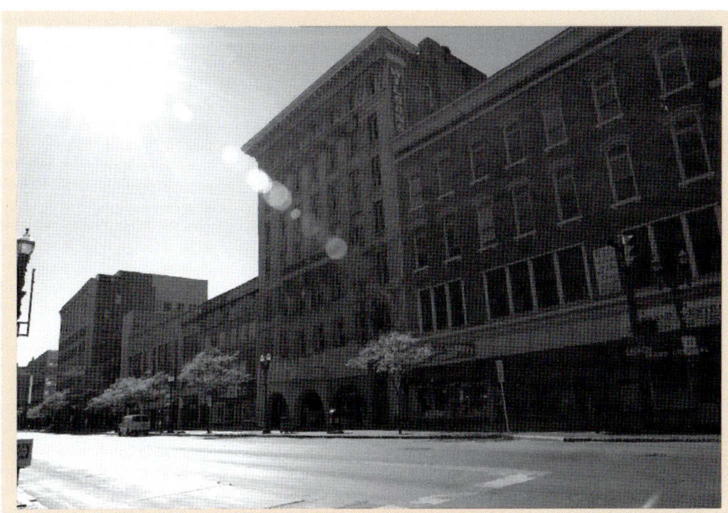

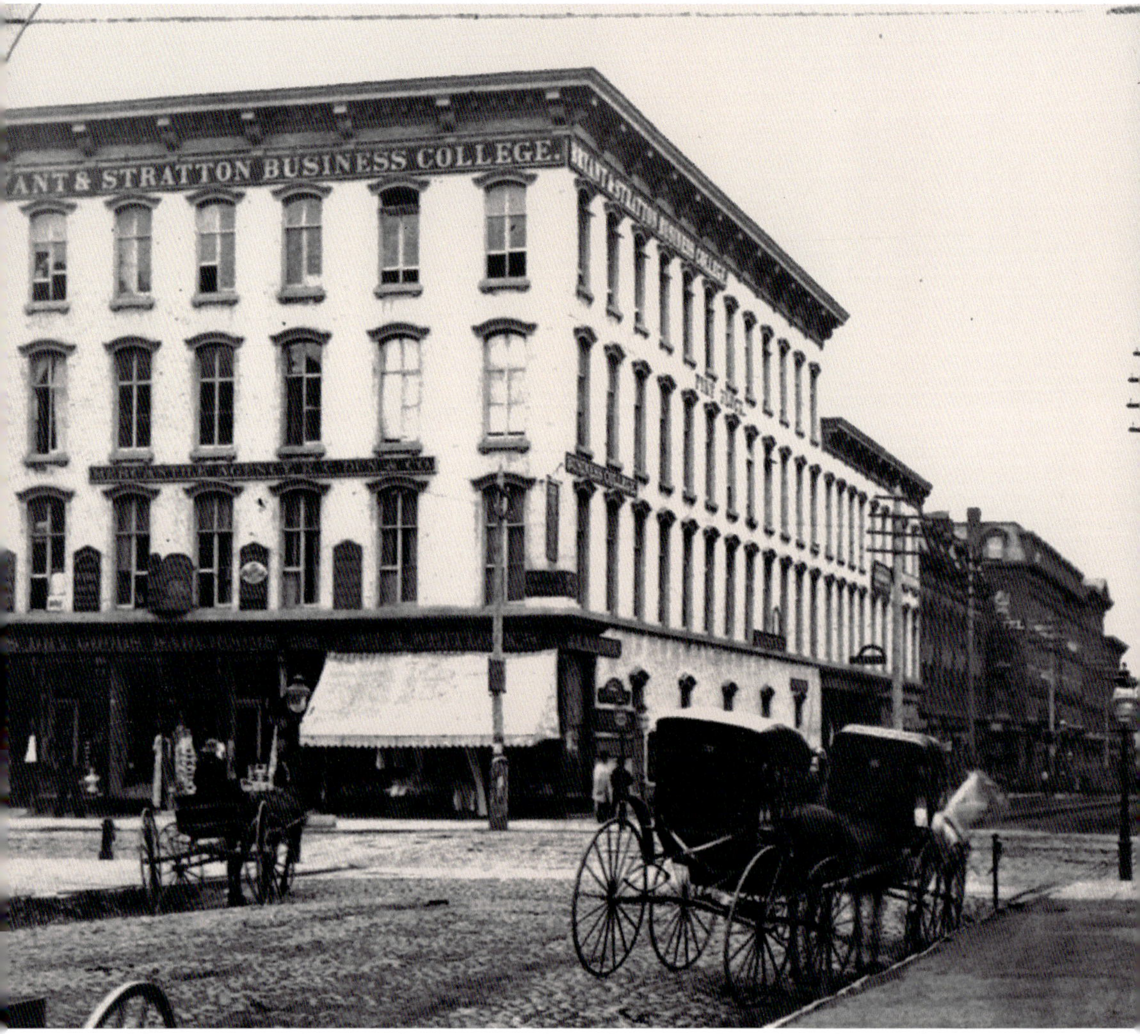

The oldest building on the block is the 1855 Italianate-style Pike Block. Retail has always occupied the first floor, and the upper floors have been offices. In this *c.* 1880 photograph, Bryant and Stratton Business College occupies the upper floors.

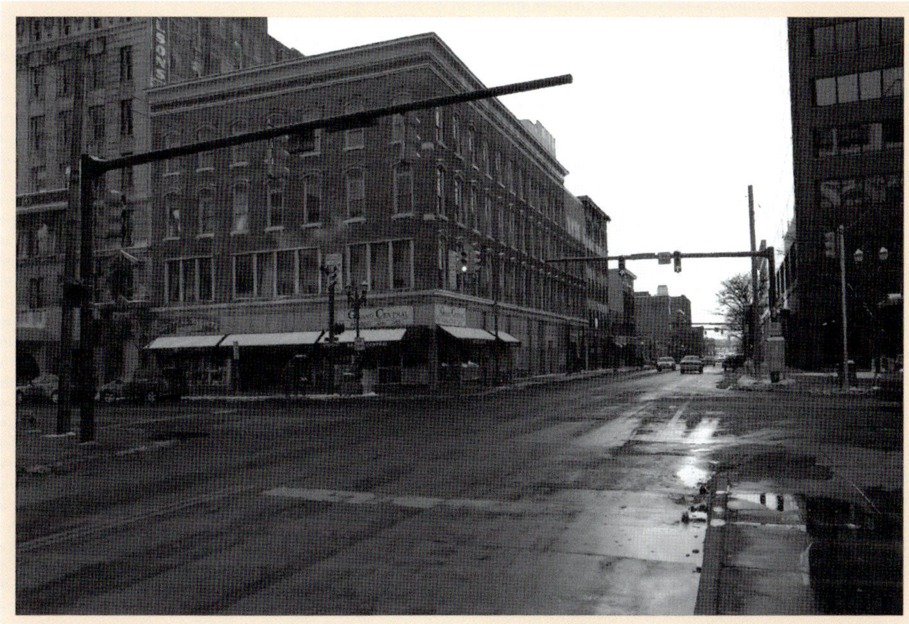

Witherill Dry Goods became the owner of the Pike Block in 1894. Witherill's became one of the major department stores. In the *c.* 1960 photograph, the building was modernized with a contemporary facade. It was removed in the 1980s.

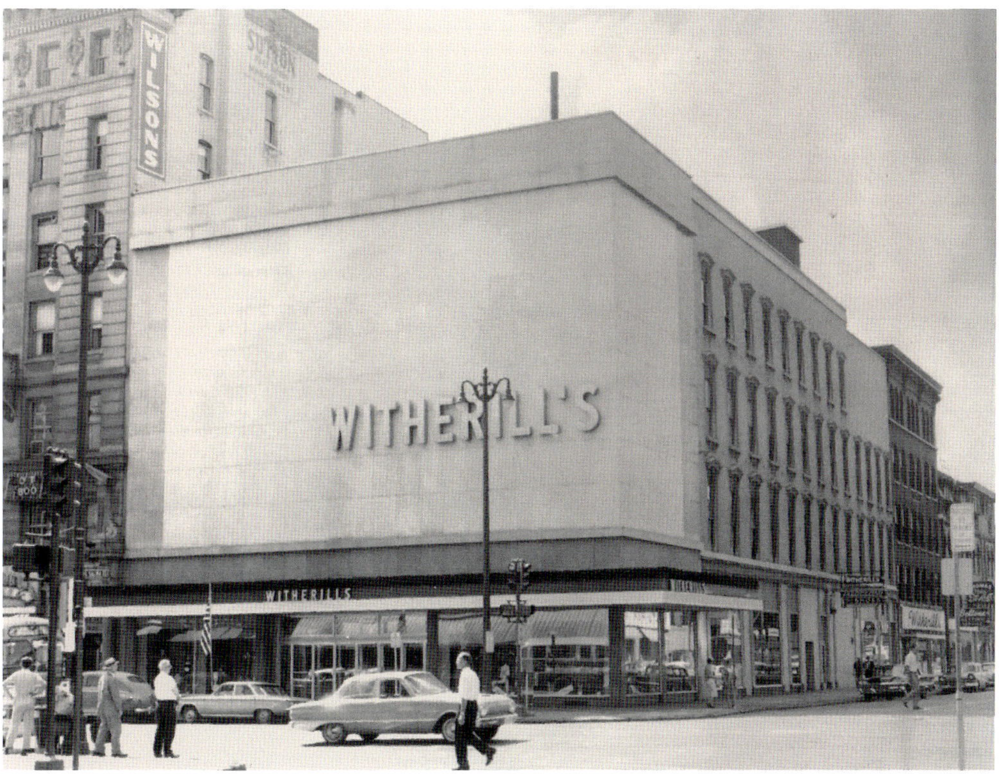

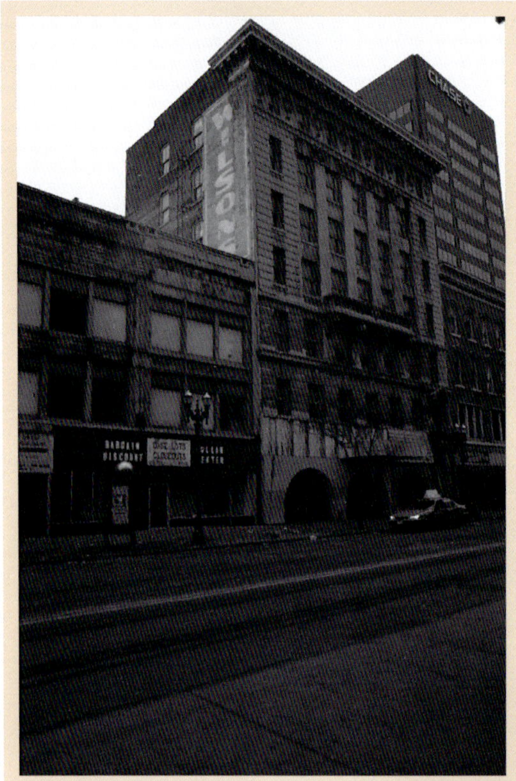

The Beaux-Arts style Wilson Building (built in 1898) was designed by Charles E. Colton as the Dillaye Memorial Building. It became known as the Wilson Building when it was purchased in 1943 by Wilson Jewelers. The 1950s photograph shows the successful jewelers expanding into the Bond Building next door. The Wilson Building is at the heart of a four-building rehabilitation project beginning in 2010, with 75 apartments and retail on the first floor.

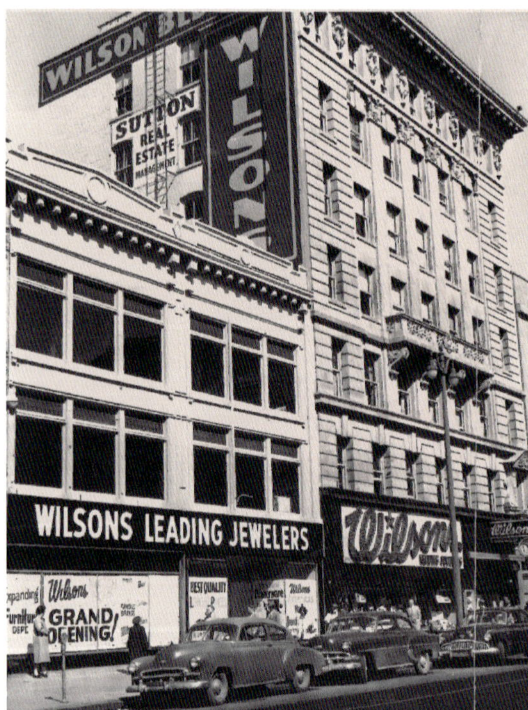

Mangel's Women's Apparel, seen in this *c.* 1935 photograph, was located in the southern bay of the Bond Building. Mangel's was a very important and successful women's clothing store. It occupied all three floors of the Bond Building bay. While the street-level facade has been completely altered, the upper floor's facade materials and windows are intact.

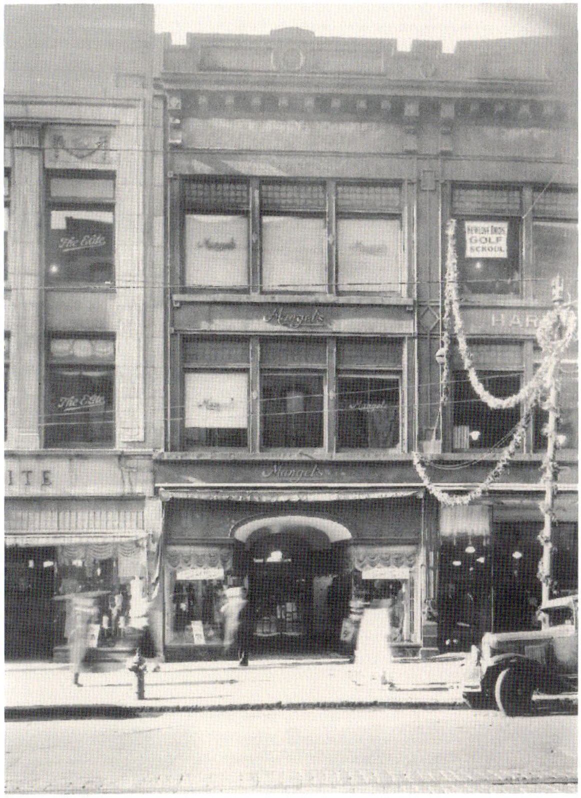

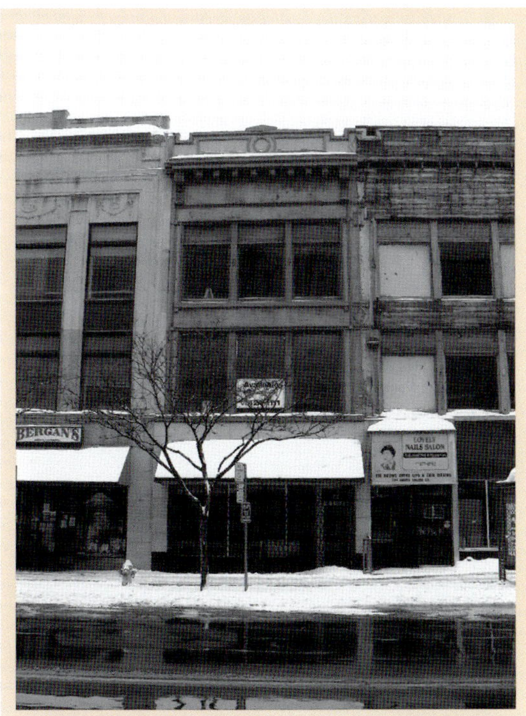

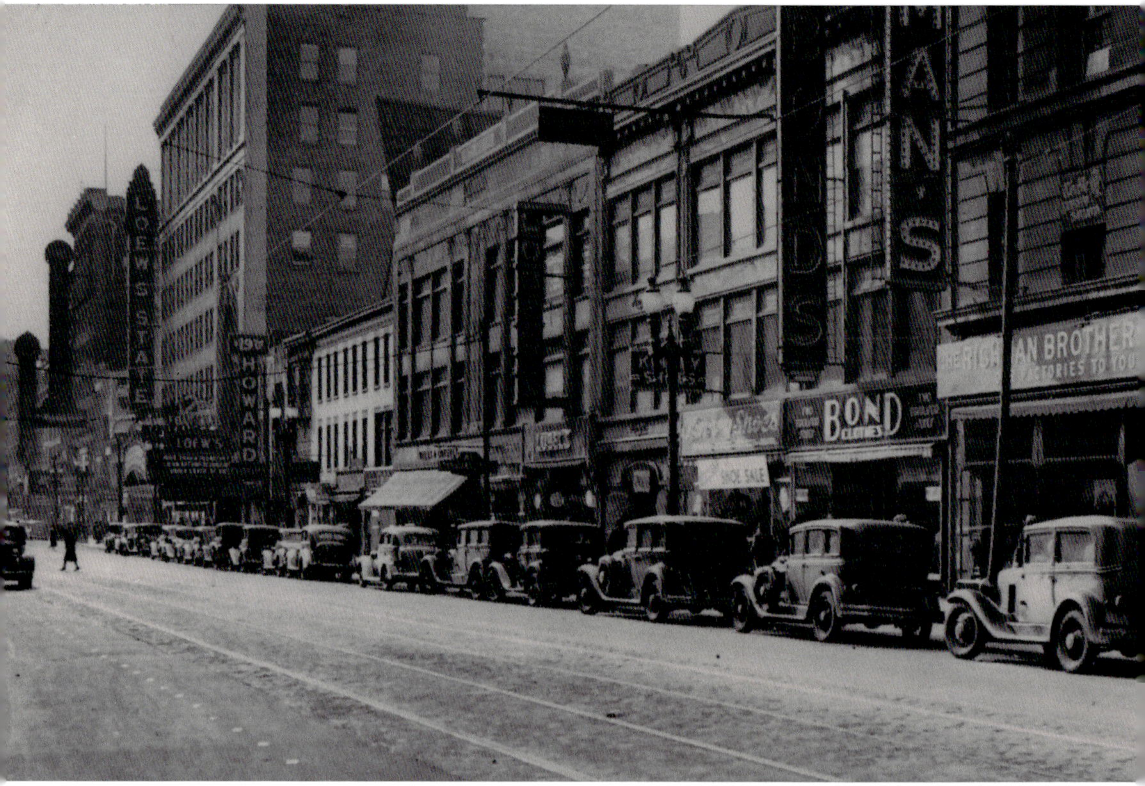

In this 1936 photograph of the west side of South Salina Street, the shorter buildings between the Wilson Building and Loew's State Theater are filled with shops selling men's and women's clothing and shoes. The Loew's was showing *More than a Secretary* and *Under Cover of Night*. The Bond Building is one of the four buildings in the Wilson Building rehabilitation project.

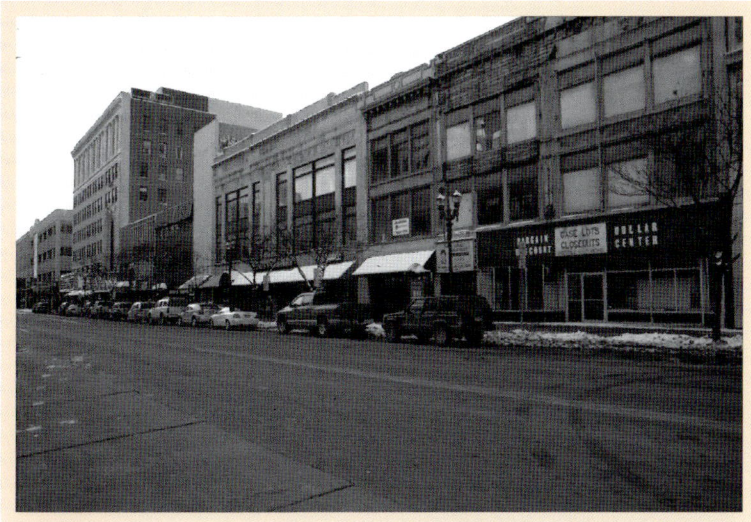

The Bond Building, the darker building on the right in this 1944 photograph, and the Betts Building, the light building to the left, were originally one building—the Butler Block, built around 1878. About 1920, the Butler Block was separated into two buildings and each was given a new facade. The Bond Building was sheathed in copper, much of which has been ripped off. The facade of the Betts Building was limestone.

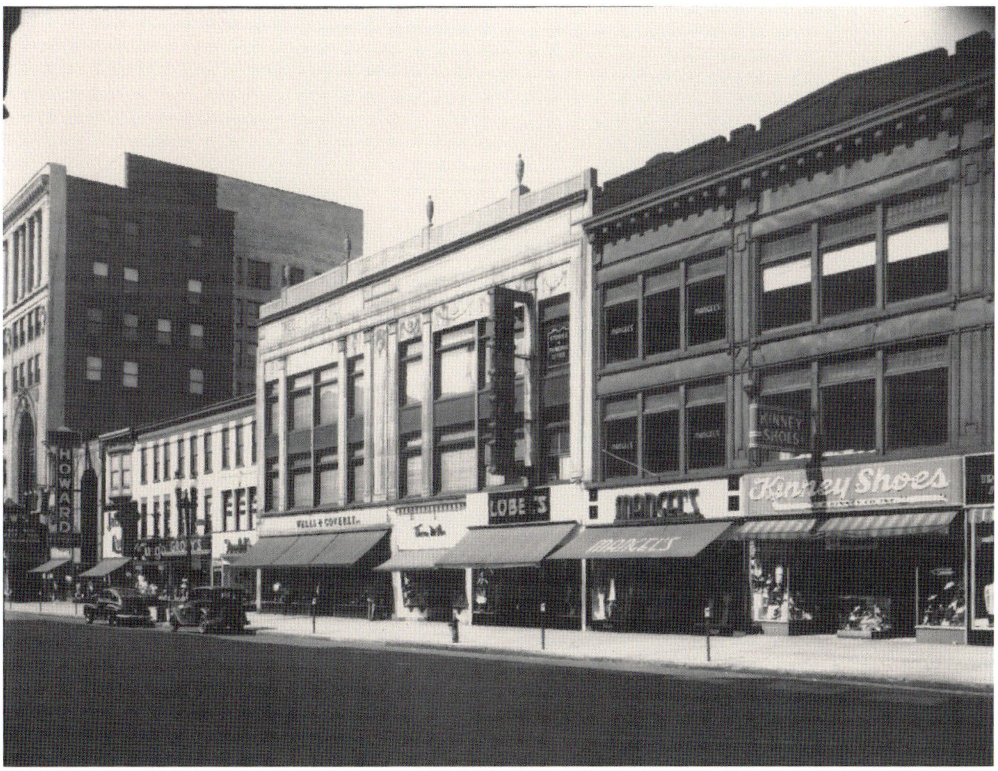

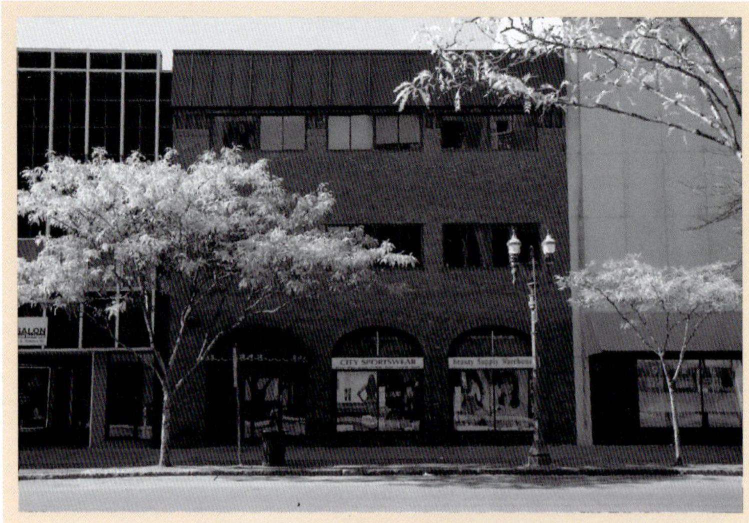

The two modest three-story buildings seen in this *c.* 1960 photograph housed Sporting Goods Company and Endicott Johnson Shoes, two important retailers on South Salina Street. These buildings were demolished in the 1970s and replaced with the existing brick building with first-floor arches. While this building is in the new historic district, it is a noncontributing building.

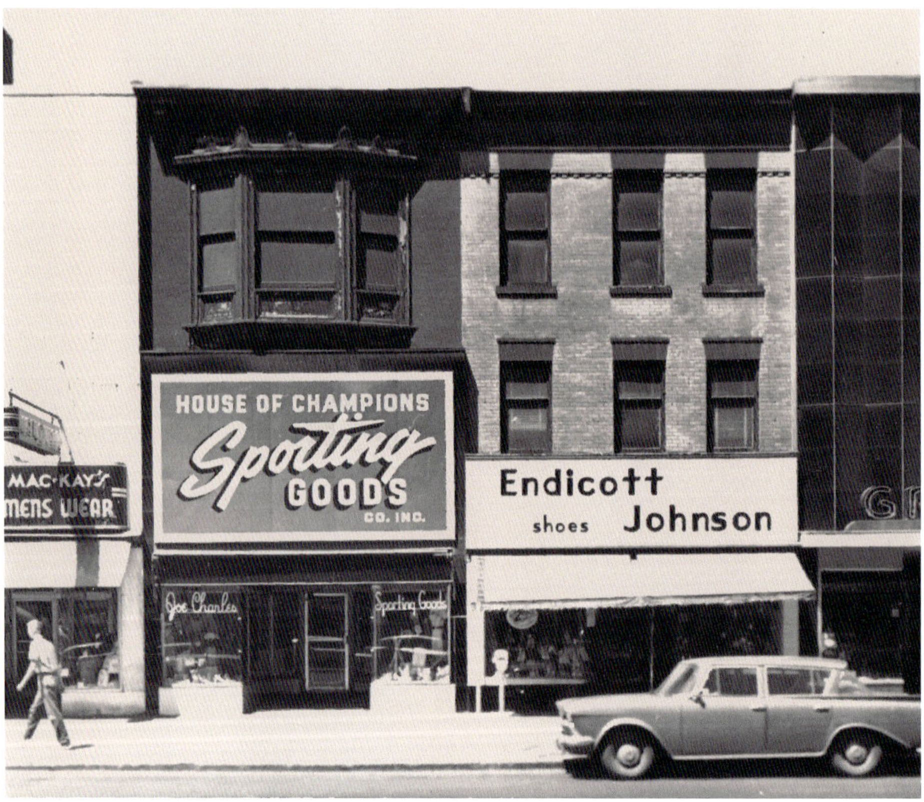

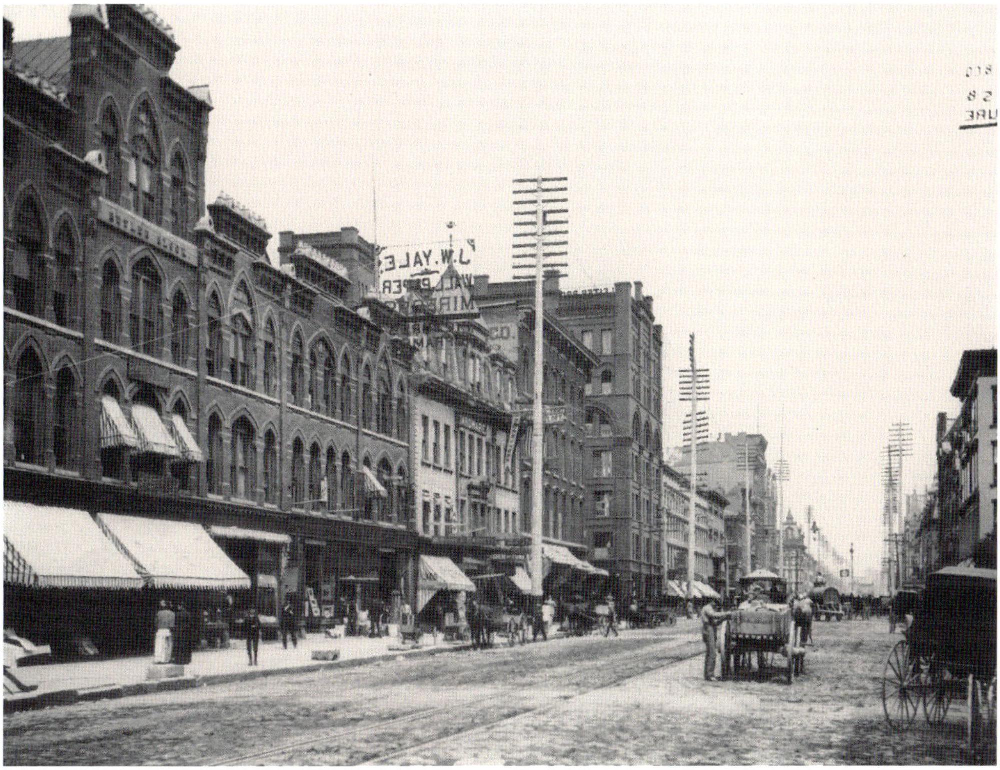

This 1890s photograph shows the west side of South Salina Street. The large building on the left was the Butler Block, designed by Horatio Nelson White around 1878. About 1920, the building was redesigned by Charles D. Wilsey and divided into two buildings with completely new facades. The Betts Building has classical detailing and is limestone. The Bond Building has copper sheeting on its facade. Both buildings have altered first-floor facades, but the upper floors are fairly intact.

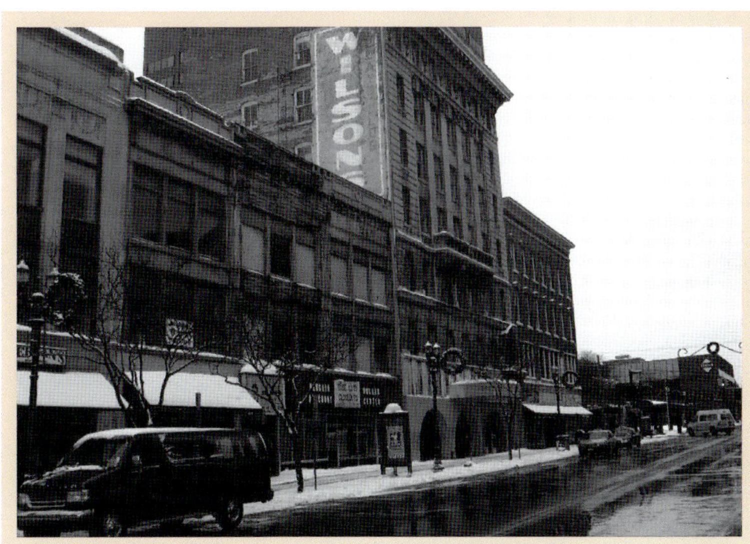

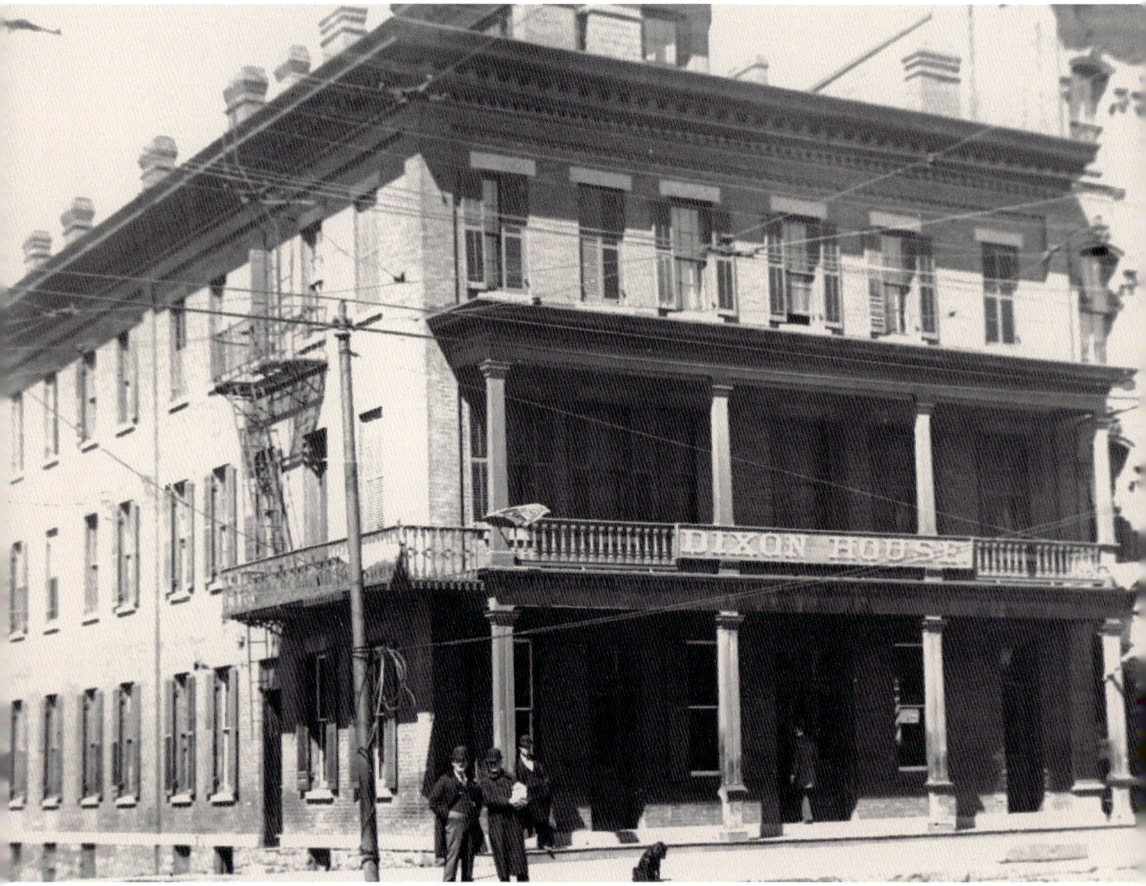

The northwest corner of South Salina and West Jefferson Streets was first occupied by the hotel Dixon House, as seen in this early-1900s photograph.

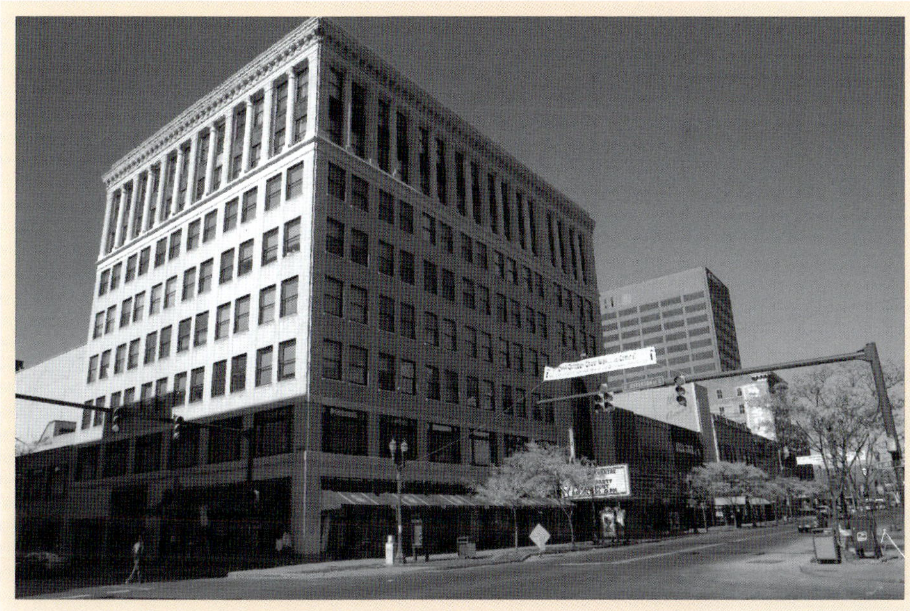

The Jefferson Hotel was constructed in the early 1920s. After it too was demolished, in 1928 this corner became the site of one of the grandest buildings in Syracuse—Loew's State Theater, designed by Thomas W. Lamb. The building contained retail on the first floor, with offices on the upper seven floors. At the center of the building was the 3,300-seat theater, decorated with Moorish, Indian, and Hindu influences. The office tower is being rehabilitated into 24 condominium units.

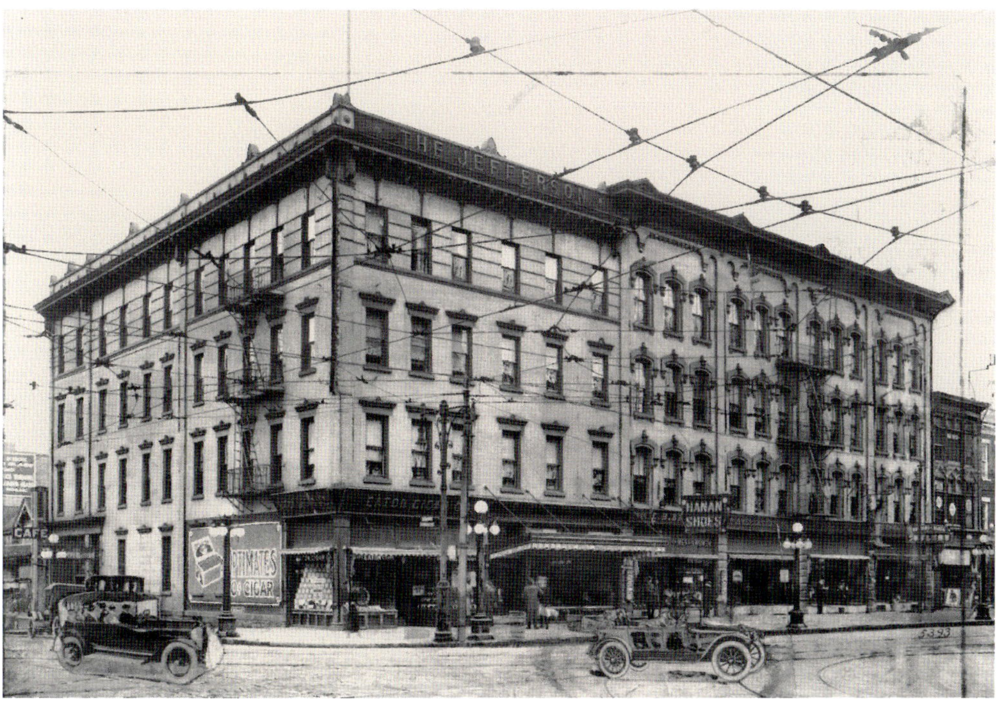

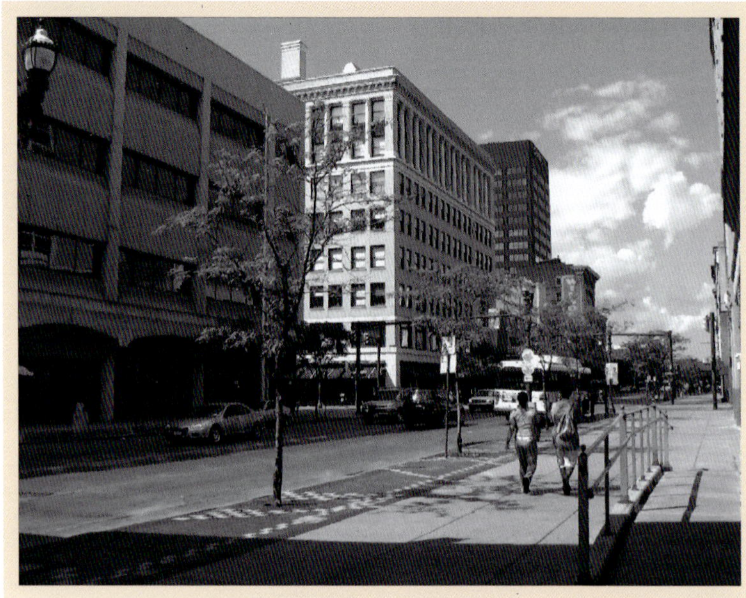

Downtown was the home of eight movie palaces. In this 1954 photograph, the RKO Keith's theater is seen across West Jefferson Street from Loew's. Keith's was demolished in the 1970s for Sibley's Department Store, which is now an office building. Loew's is the only theater remaining. In 1977, the interior of the theater was to be demolished for a parking garage. A rescue committee was formed and saved the theater. Today it is operated by a nonprofit group.

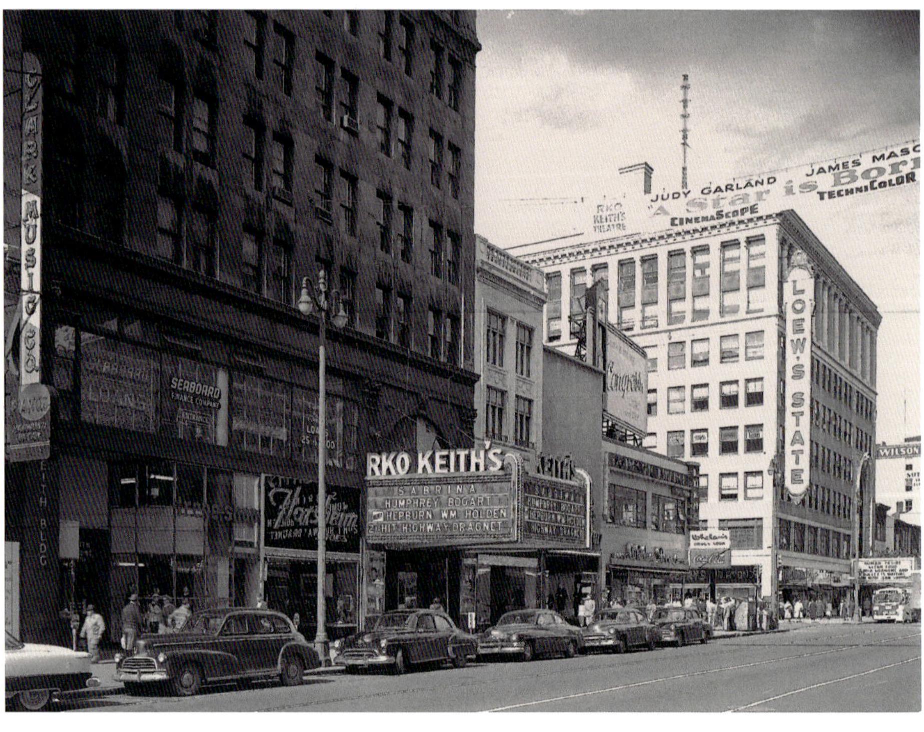

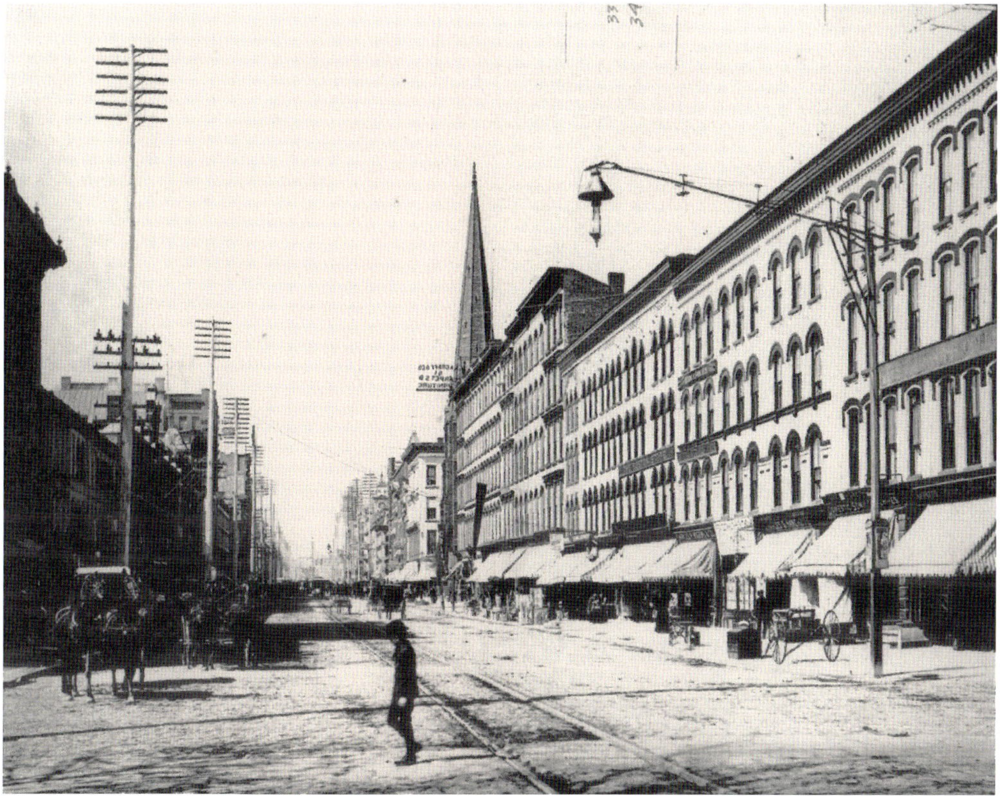

Looking north on the east side of South Salina Street, this 1890s photograph shows a variety of three- and four-story Italianate buildings. The church at the corner is architect Minard LeFever's 1849 First Presbyterian Church, demolished in 1905. The Woolworth Building is now at this location. The seven-story building north of West Fayette Street in the contemporary photograph is the 1894 McCarthy Building by Charles E. Colton. It was the home of one of the major department stores.

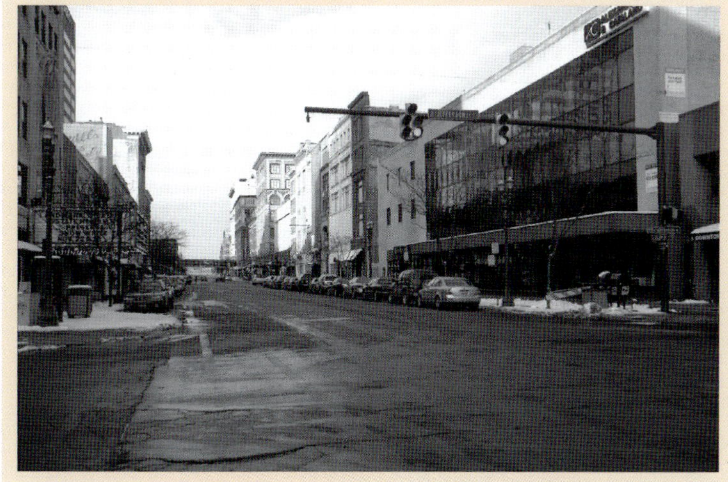

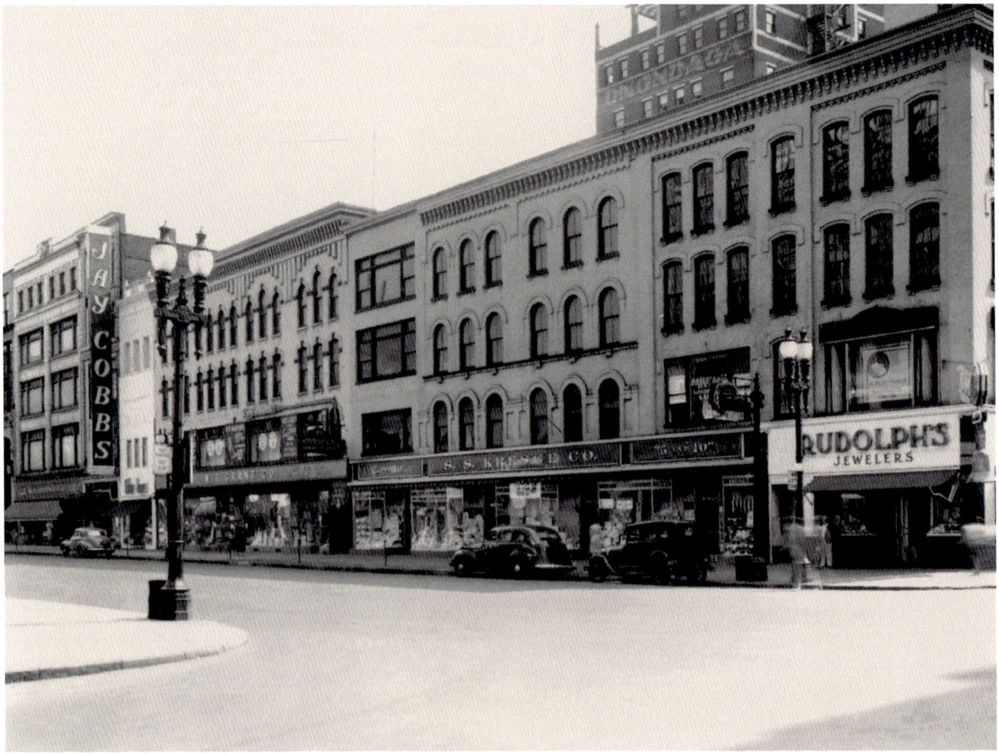

The 1940s photograph shows the beginning of the transformation of the east side of the 300 block. Some of the early Italianate buildings remain; however, the first floors have been modified, and in some, the second-story windows have been replaced by larger ones. The newer buildings also have large upper-floor windows. The second building is the home of the S. S. Kresge Company five-and-dime. By 1950, the block was completely transformed. S. S. Kresge's new 1949 building is now an office building.

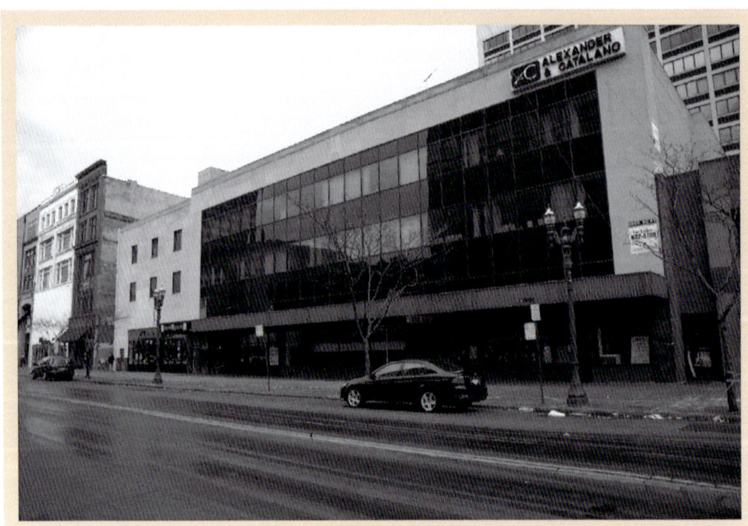

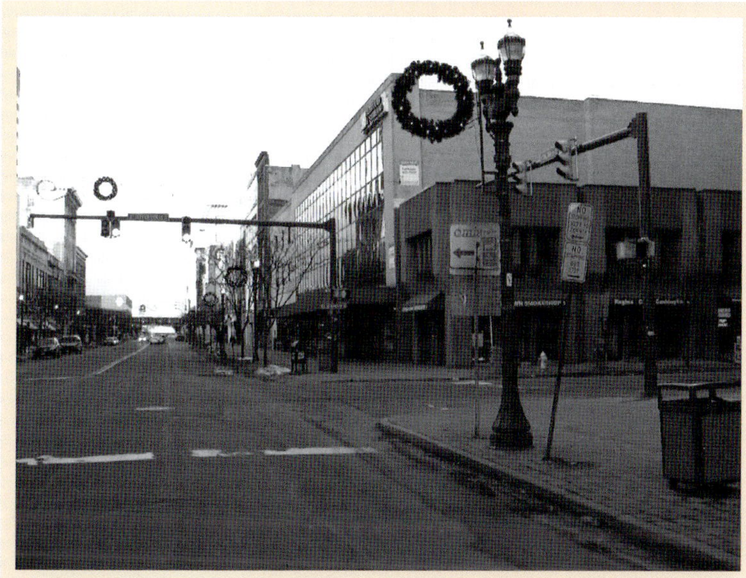

Syracuse is known as the "snow capital" of cities in the United States with a population of over 100,000. The 1930s photograph taken at the corner of South Salina and Jefferson Streets illustrates why the city has this title. The record snowfall in Syracuse was during the 1992–1993 season, when the city received 192.1 inches. The normal snowfall is 111.9 inches.

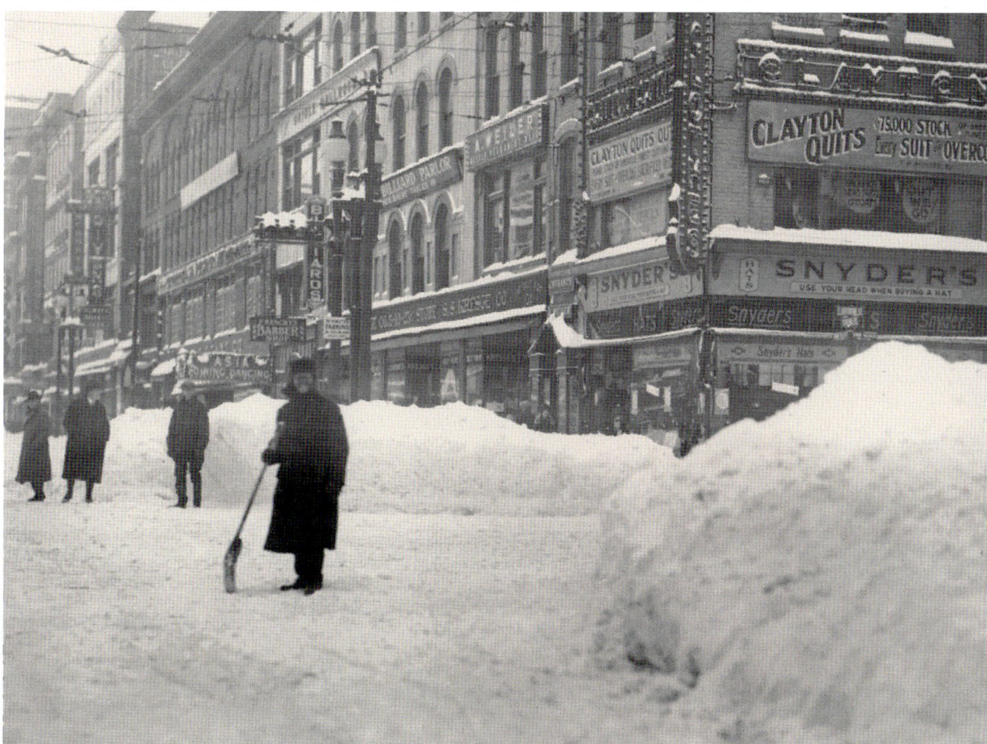

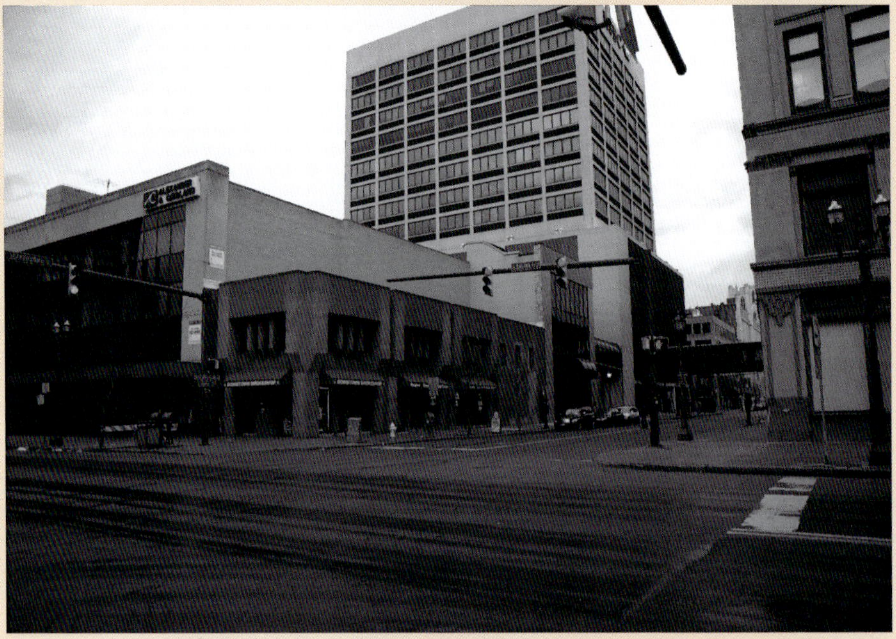

This *c.* 1970 photograph of the corner of South Salina and East Jefferson Streets shows the 1949 S. S. Kresge building, which had become a Kmart at the time of this photograph. Rudolph's Jewelers still exists on the corner, but the four-story building has had the top two floors removed. The contemporary photograph shows the extensive alterations to the Kmart building, which took place in the 1980s. The grand Onondaga Hotel on Warren Street was demolished in 1970.

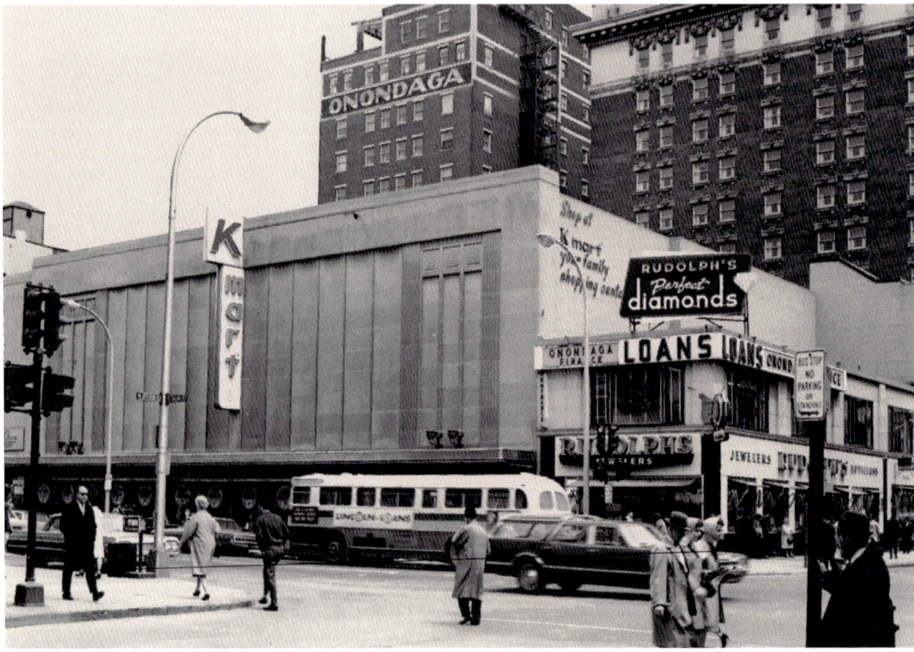

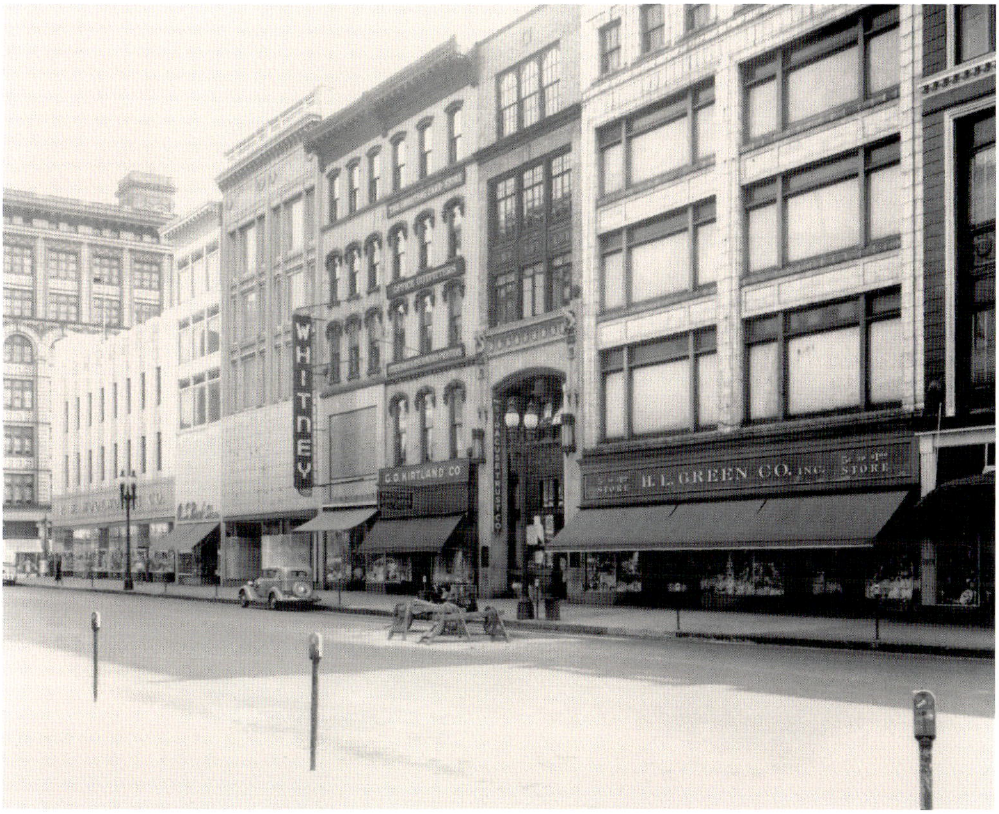

This *c.* 1945 photograph shows the further transformation of the east side of South Salina Street. All buildings have been replaced, except for Whitney's and the G. D. Kirtland Company building, and their facades have been particularly altered. The prominent H. L. Green Company, a 5¢ to $1 store, is on the right. The contemporary photograph shows the further alterations of the store facades.

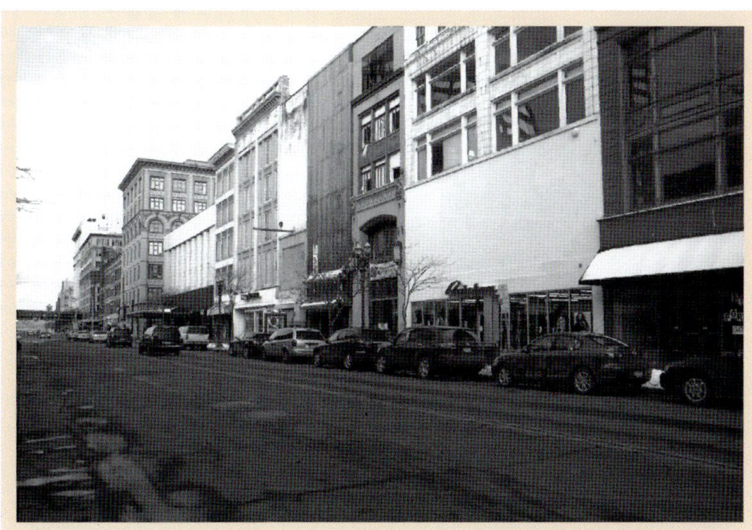

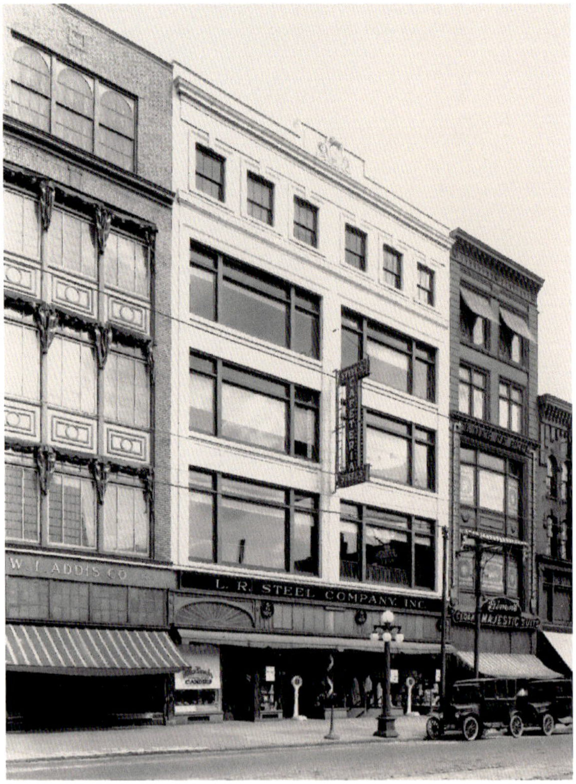

In the *c.* 1925 and contemporary photographs, three of the most important buildings on the east side of South Salina Street can be seen. From left to right are the Peatfield Building, built around 1900; the L. R. Steele Company building, built during the second decade of the 20th century; and the Jay Cobb Store building, built about 1919. The Peatfield first housed W. I. Addis, women's clothing, and later the Syracuse Trust Company. The first two stories of the building were altered around the 1920s.

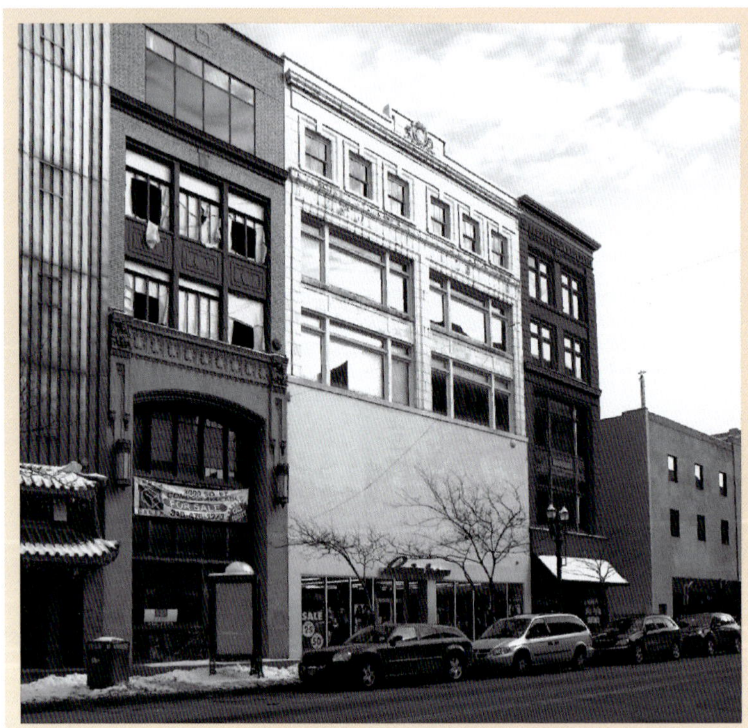

These photographs of 321 and 323 South Salina Street record the history of almost 150 years of change. The *c.* 1925 photograph shows that the mid-1800s Italianate building of the G. D. Kirtland Company as well as the Park-Brannock Company building have had their first two floors altered. The owner of the Park-Brannock Company, Charles Brannock invented and patented the first scientific measuring device for the human foot in 1927 and 1928. The contemporary photograph shows both buildings covered.

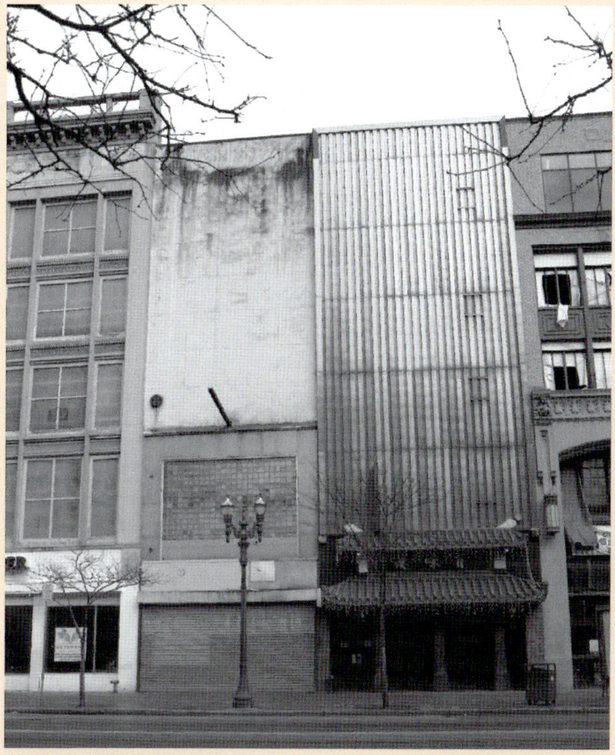

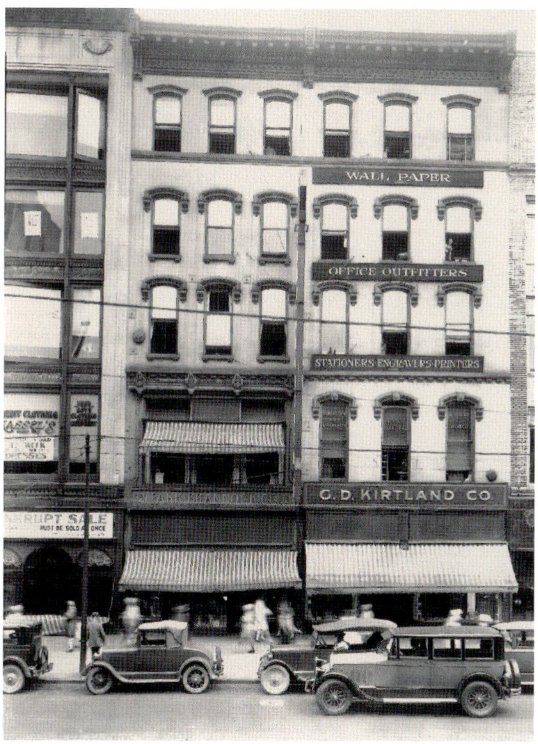

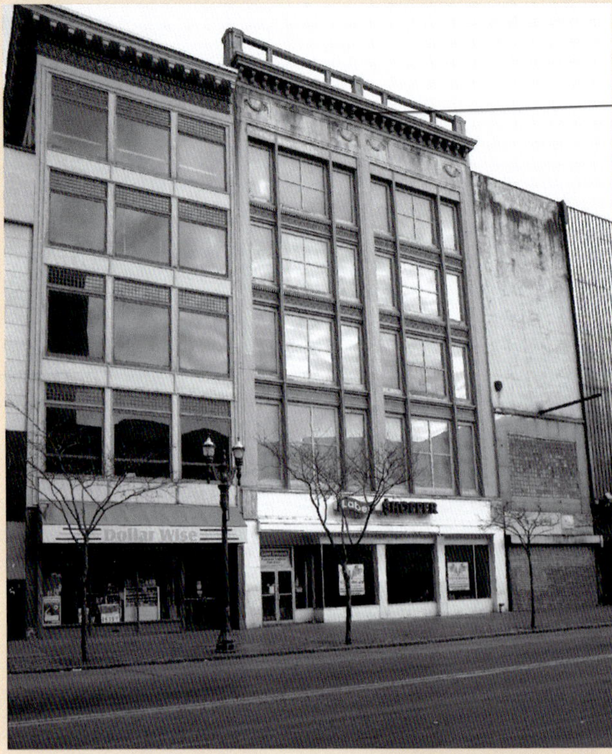

This *c.* 1915 building seen in a *c.* 1935 photograph was the home of Lerners Shops, women's apparel, and Liggets Drug Store. Both first-floor facades had been altered by the time of the photograph. The building was renovated in the 1990s with a new first-floor facade. The original large, single fix-pane upper-floor windows were replaced.

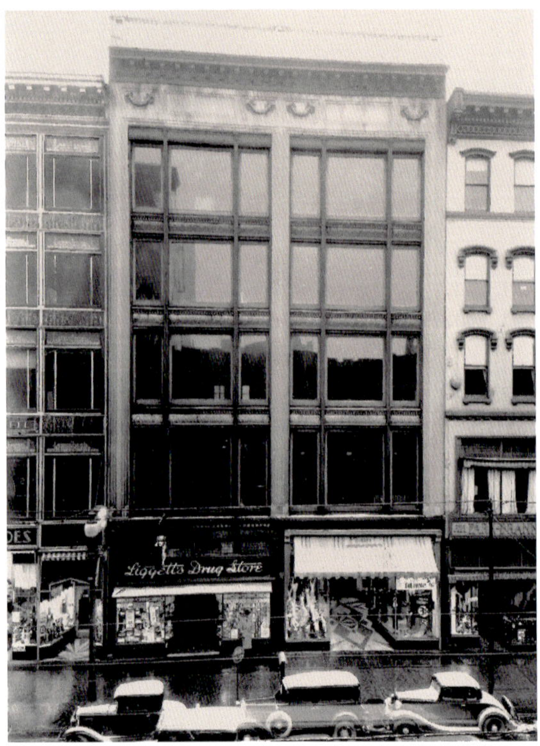

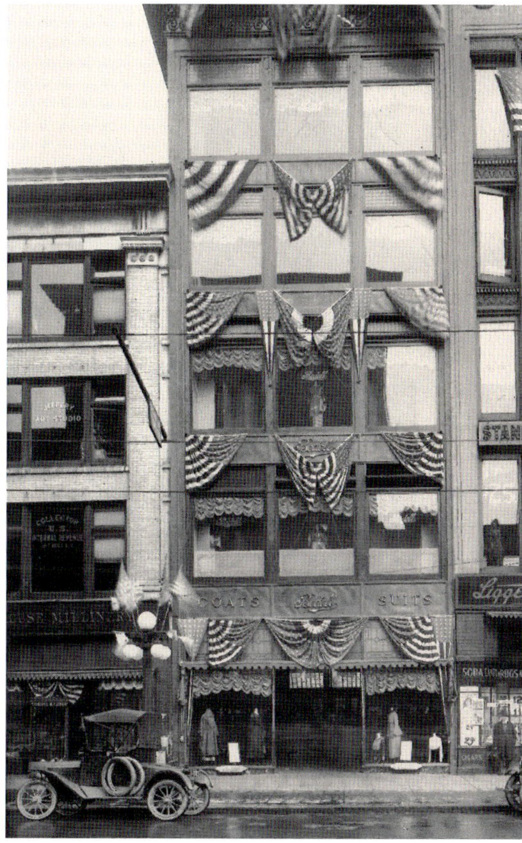

Bedell was a very important women's apparel store. It occupied all five stories of this *c.* 1856 building. In about 1915, the building was completely altered with a new facade. The only part of the original building is the cornice. The *c.* 1920 photograph shows the building decorated for some important event or holiday. Bedell had branches in Brooklyn, Newark, Philadelphia, Milwaukee, and St. Louis. The building was renovated in the 1990s with a new first-floor facade.

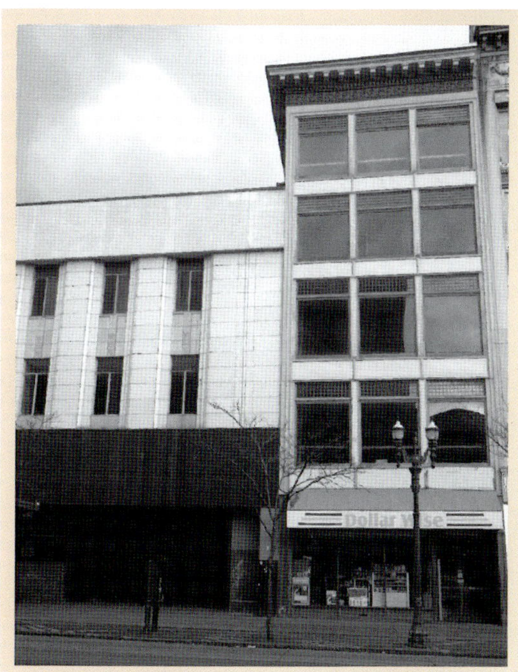

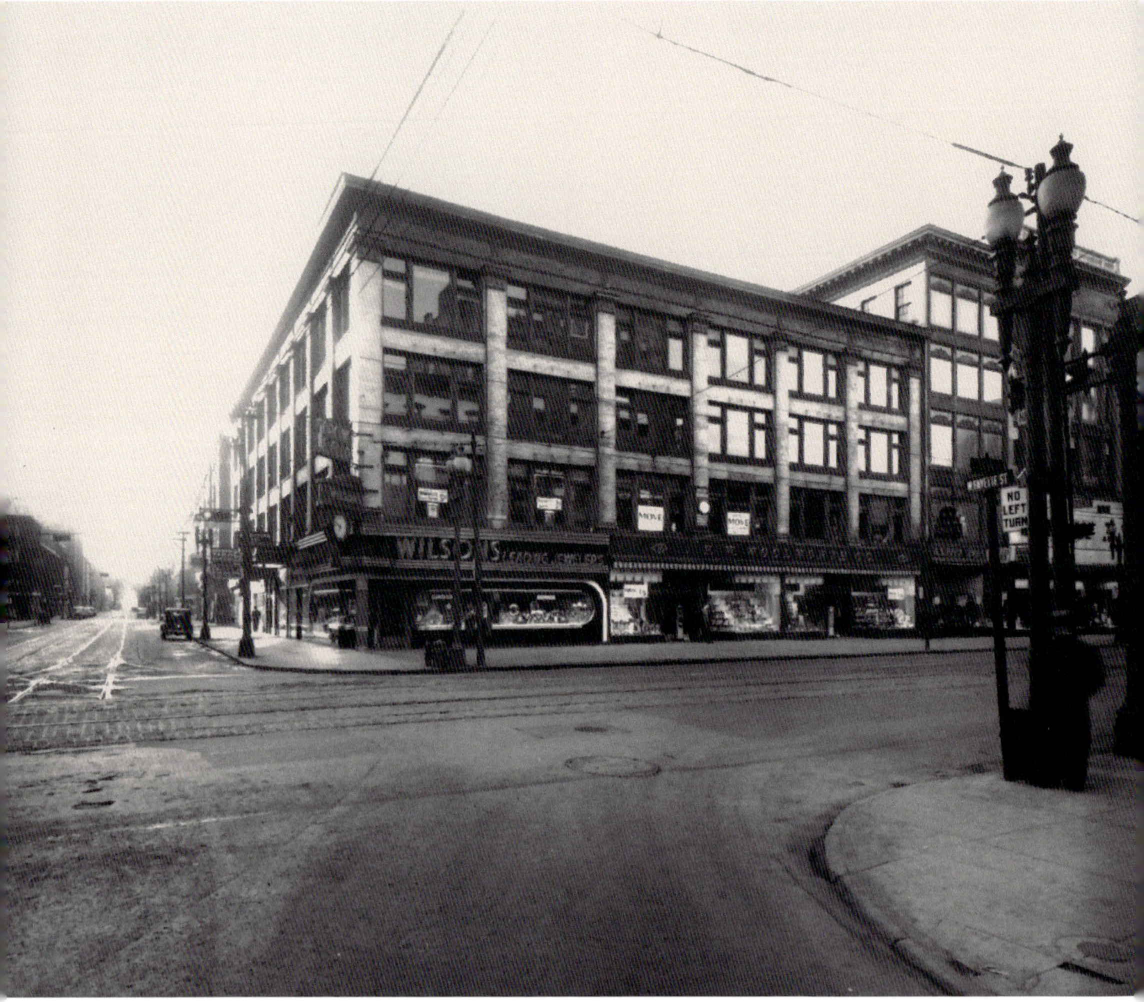

When the First Presbyterian Church was demolished in 1905, it was replaced with the commercial building seen in this *c.* 1935 photograph. The building was home to F. W. Woolworth Company and Wilson Jewelers. By the time of the photograph, Wilson Jewelers had a new art moderne–style storefront.

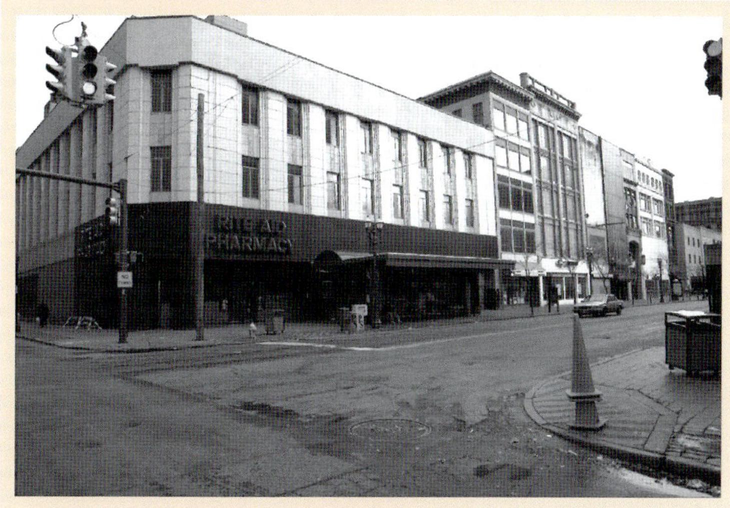

The commercial building built in the early 20th century was demolished and replaced with a 1941 art deco–style building, which housed Woolworth's. The art deco building's first floor and parapet were modified in the 1980s. It now is a Rite Aid Pharmacy.

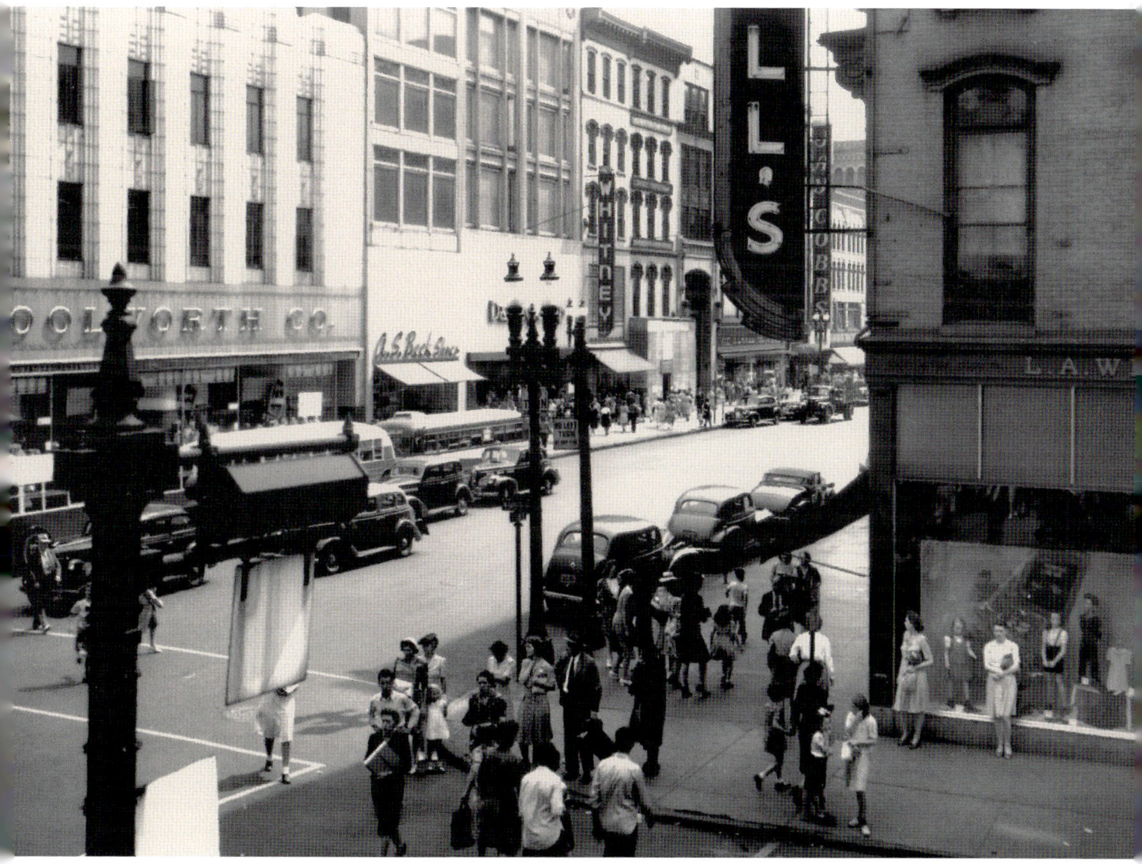

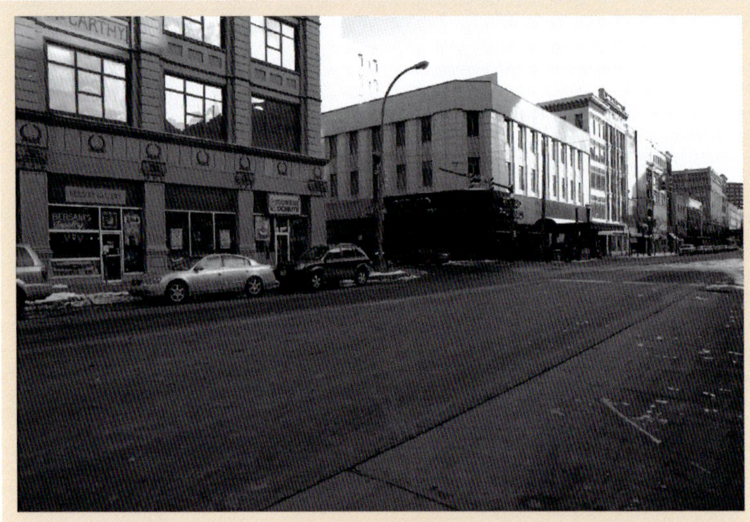

This pair of photographs, looking south on South Salina Street and taken just over 50 years apart, clearly illustrates the transformation of the main street of downtown Syracuse. The 1953 photograph shows the Lincoln Stores department store in the McCarthy Building at the left and Dey Brothers department store at the right side. In between the two are Woolworth's, Kresge's, and a variety of other retail stores. The contemporary photograph shows South Salina Street ready for the planned redevelopment projects.

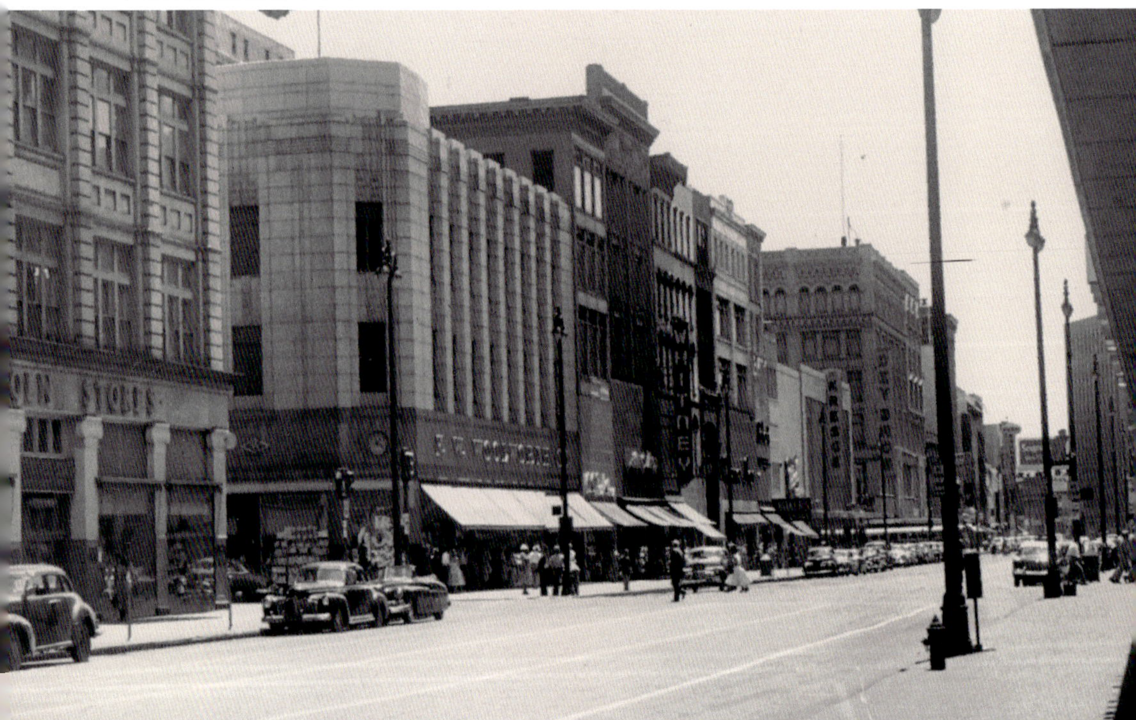

CHAPTER 6

South Clinton Street

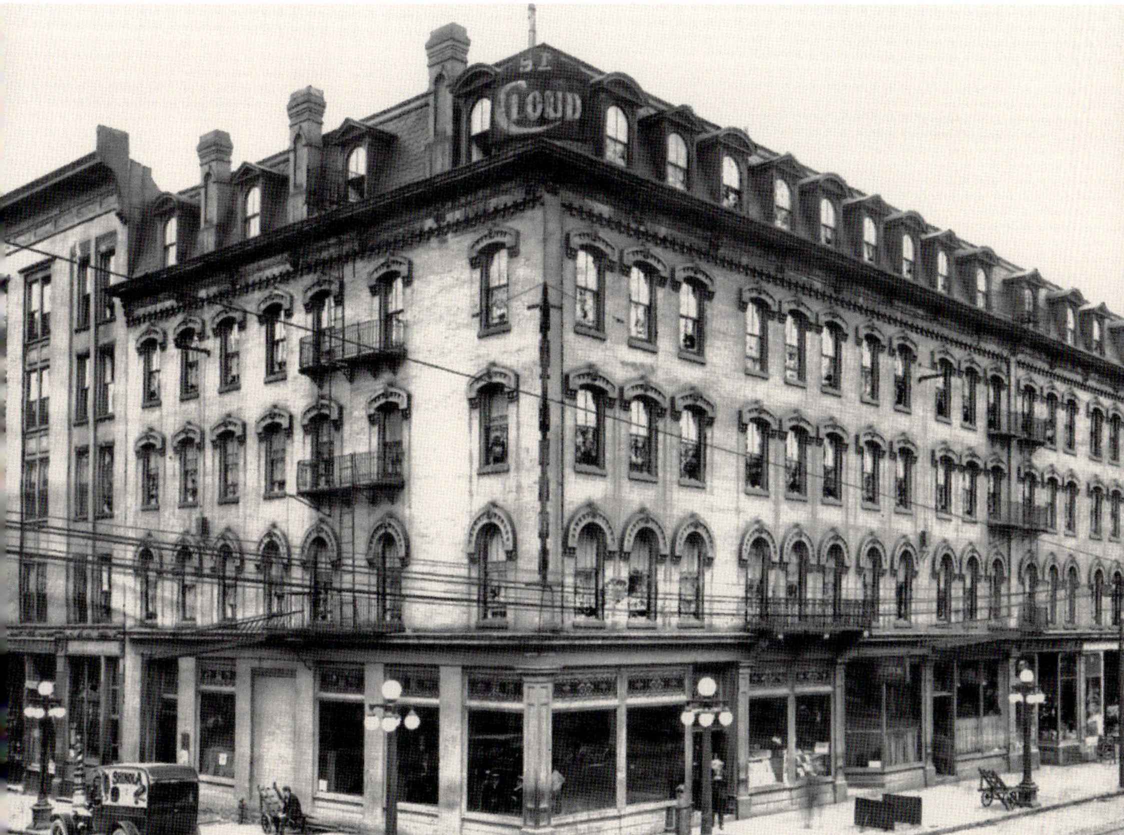

Located at the corner of South Clinton and West Fayette Streets, the St. Cloud Hotel was just a block east of the NYCRR passenger station in Armory Square. Unfortunately, the hotel was demolished in 1953, and now only a parking lot remains where this grand structure once stood.

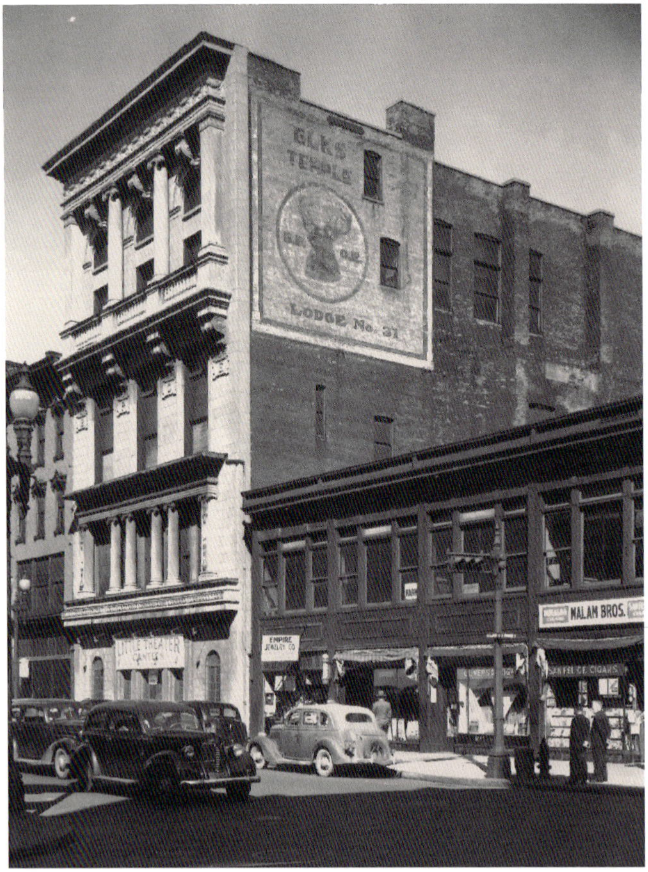

In this historic photograph taken at the corner of West Washington and South Clinton Streets, the NYCRR office building can be seen on the right. Next to that was the Lodge 31 of the Benevolent and Protective Order of Elks. Today none of the buildings seen remain. Constructed in 1974 with extensive renovations in 1982, the Atrium Building is now located on this block.

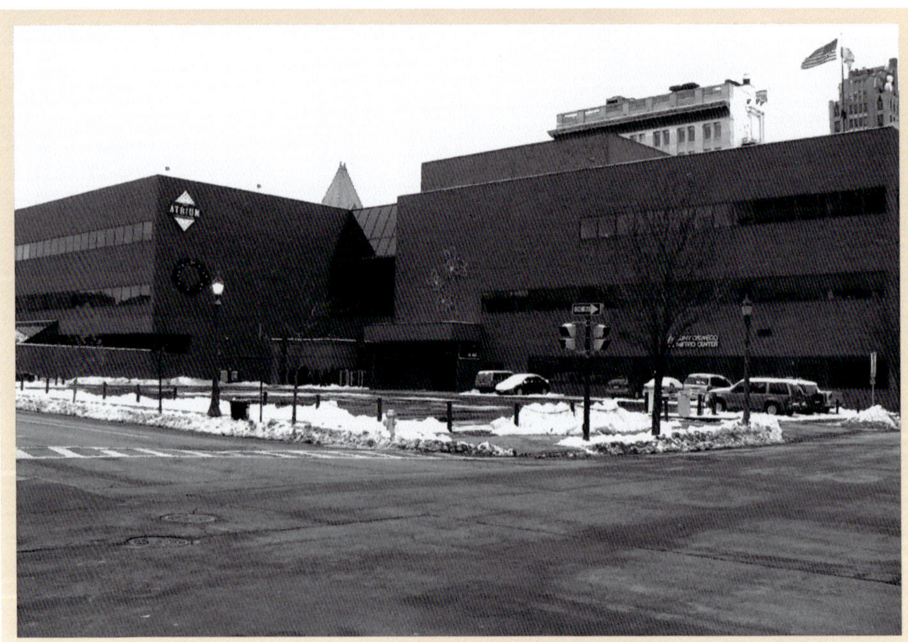

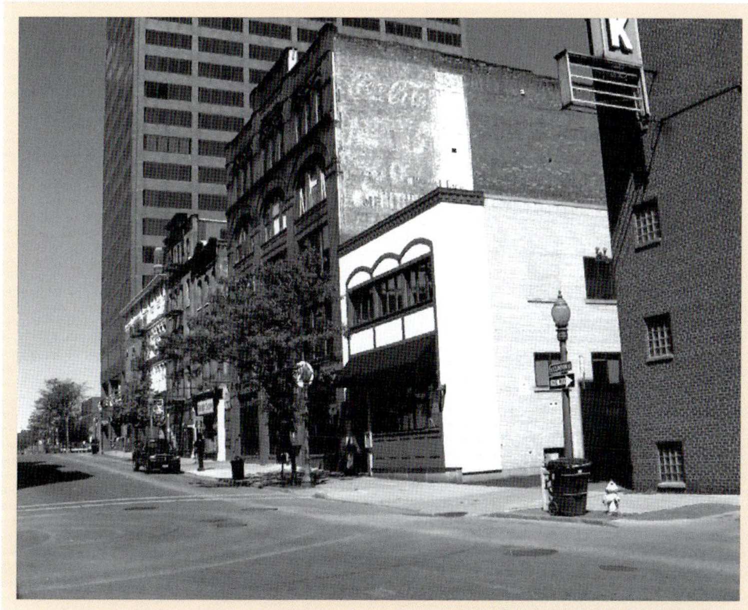

In this early-1900s photograph looking north on South Clinton Street, a number of signs for past businesses can be seen, including King Furniture Company, the Kirk Hotel, and, across West Fayette Street, O'Donnell's and the Edwards Store. Today the buildings in the foreground remain. Toward the center of both images is the Butler Building, built around 1866 with an addition in 1893.

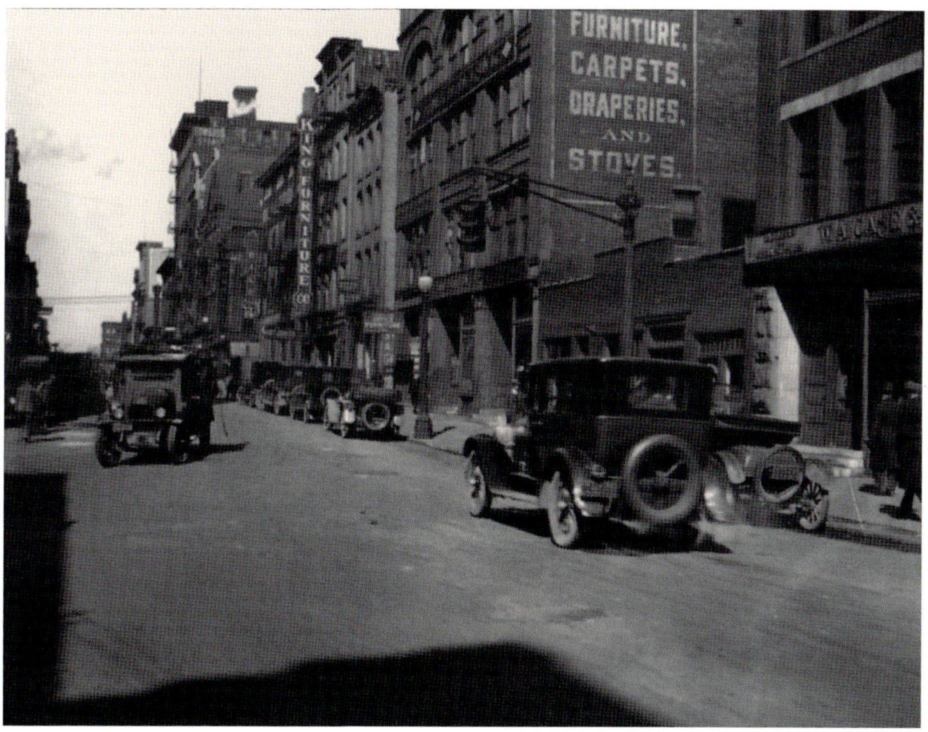

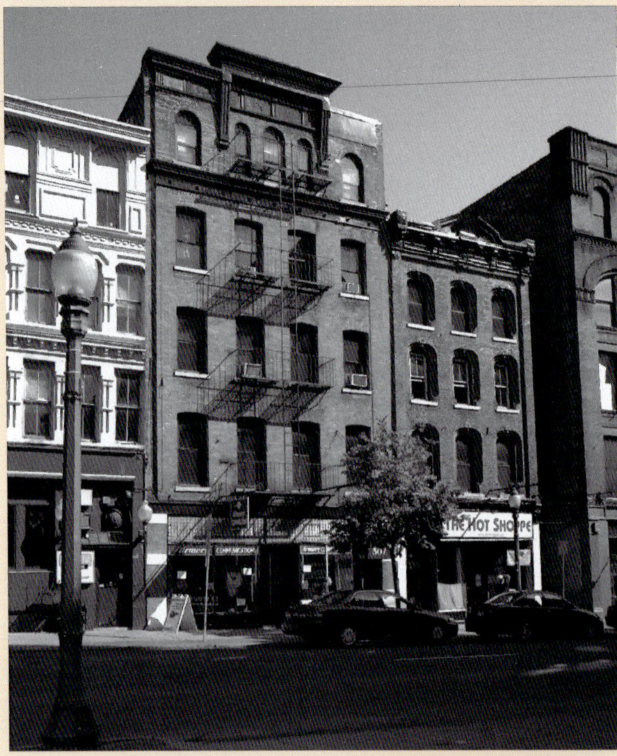

In this mid-1900s photograph, another furniture retailer was located in this building adjacent to the Kirk Hotel. The building, however, was built in the 1870s originally as a foundry. The fifth floor and cornice were added in the early 1900s. The adjacent building once housed a factory with lodging above.

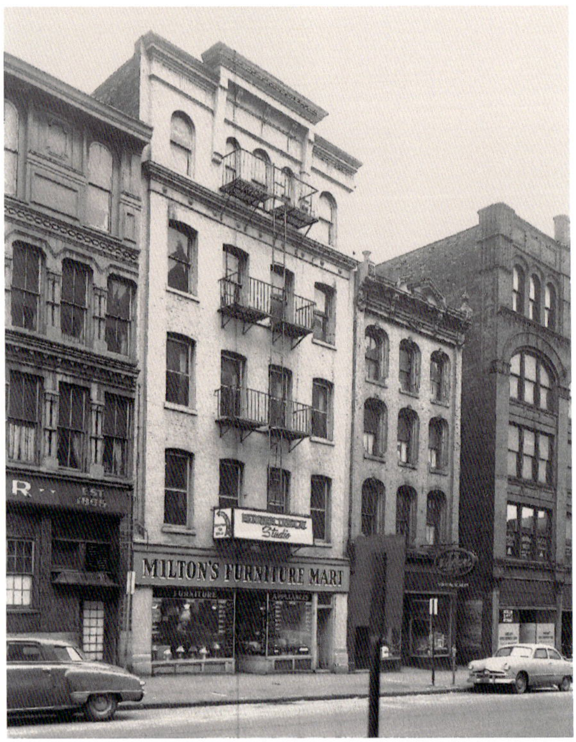

Designed by Asa L. Merrick and built in 1883, the Neal and Hyde building was a dry goods warehouse for wholesalers William Neal and Salem Hyde. In the mid-1900s, the gabled towers were removed from the roofline. Today this impressive structure still stands, and after renovations in 1999, it became the home of Syracuse Suds Factory brewpub.

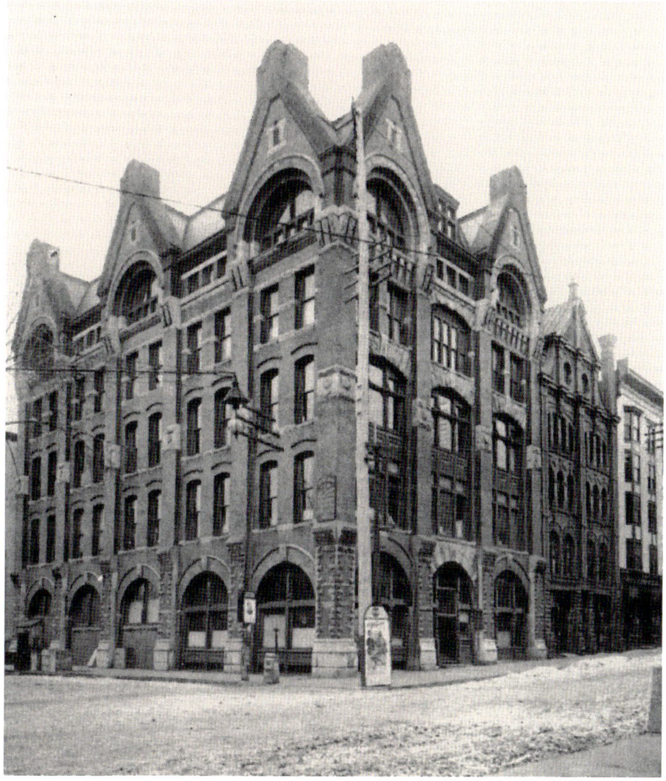

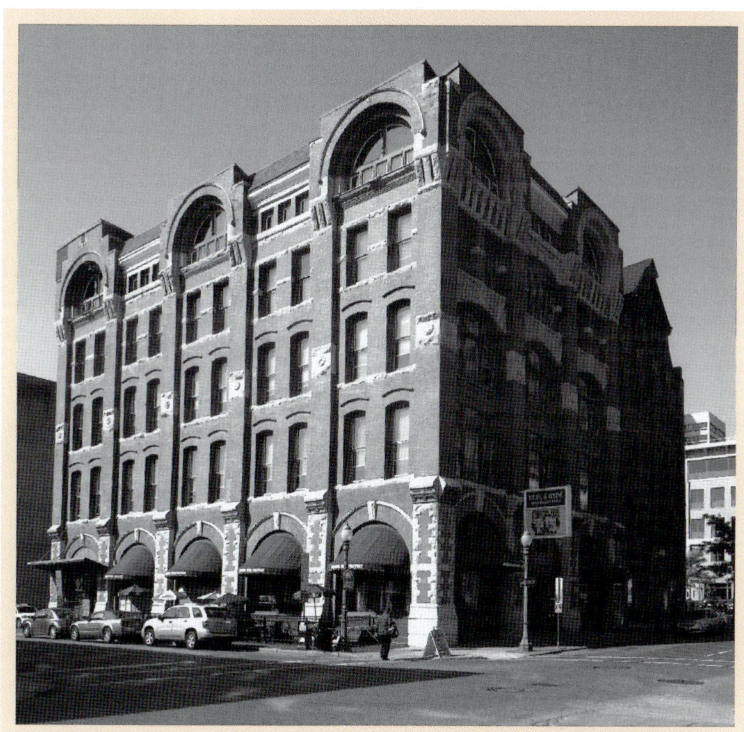

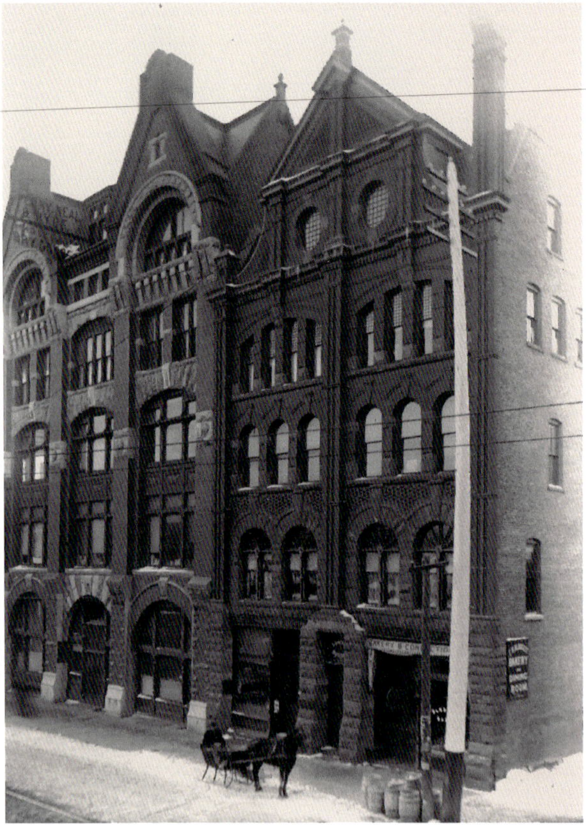

The fine Queen Anne–style Donohue Building, adjacent to the Neal and Hyde building, was constructed by Syracuse physician Florence Q. Donohue around 1885 to serve as his office and residence. After the physician's offices closed, it became a bakery—as can be seen in this photograph—with residential space above. Today the building provides office space on the upper floors with retail/restaurant space on the ground floor.

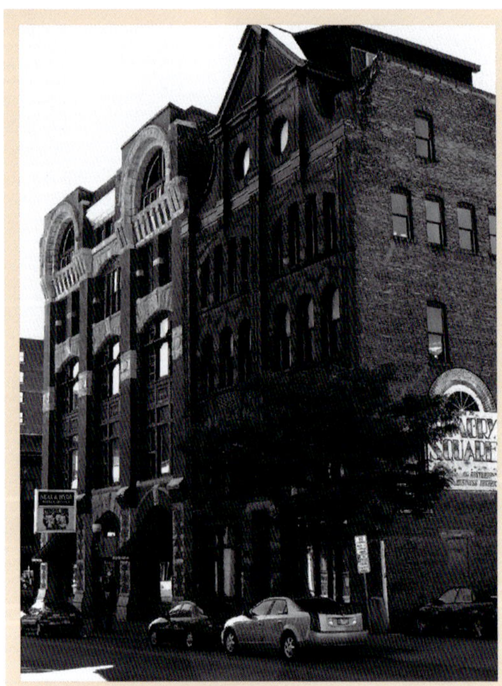

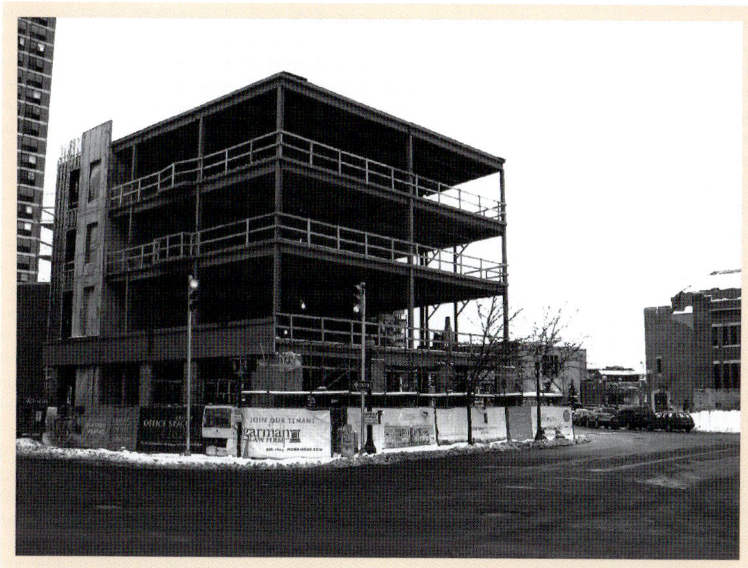

On the right in this historic photograph is the Syracuse fire engine house No. 6, which was located at the corner of West Jefferson and South Clinton Streets. In the middle was the first home for Gaylord Brothers, which opened in 1896 selling library, bank, and school supplies. Until very recently, the location on the corner was a parking lot across from the Jefferson Clinton Hotel. The new building will include condominiums, offices, and retail space.

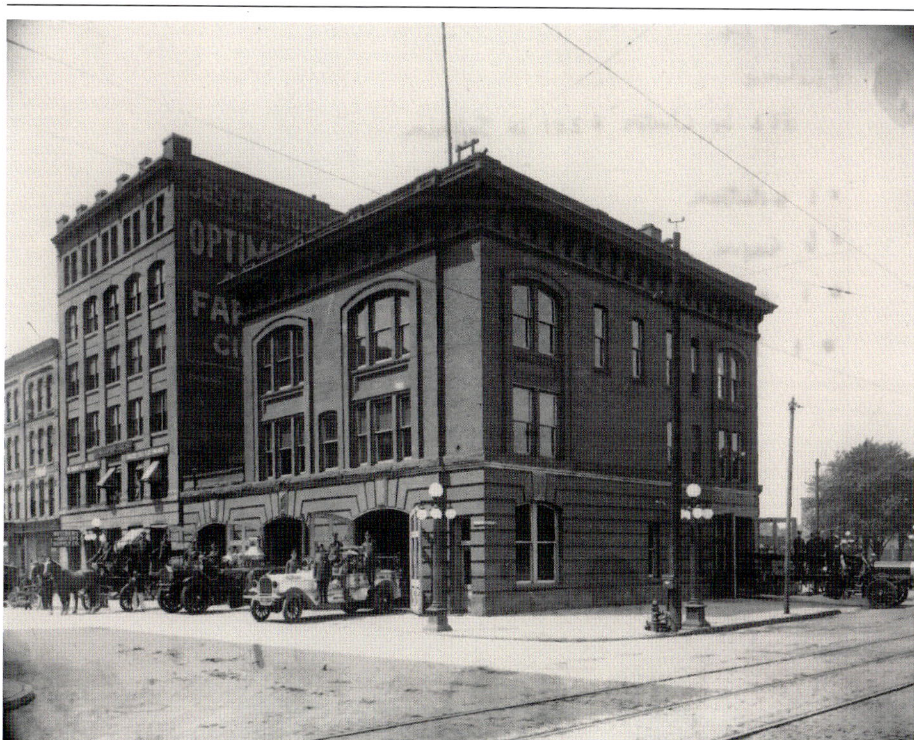

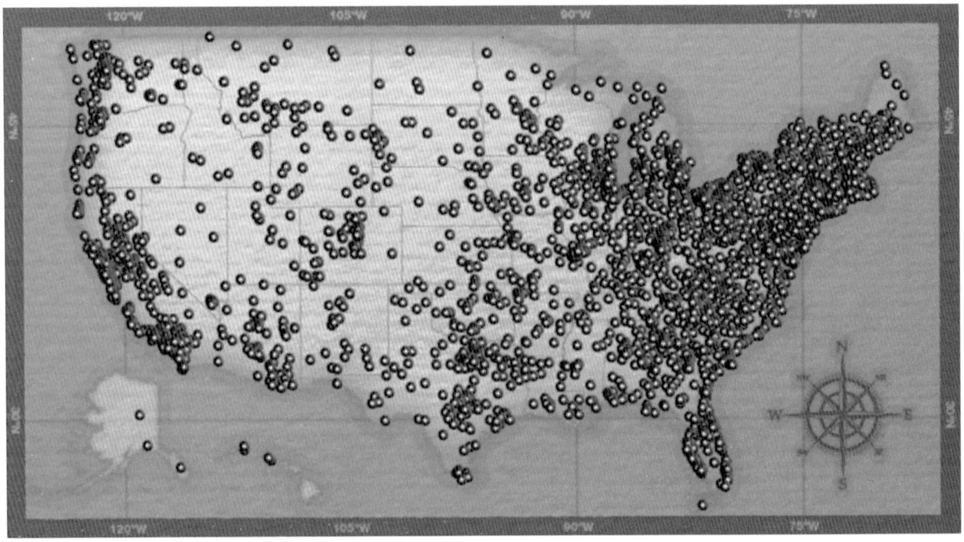

Consistent with our mission to preserve history on a local level, this book was printed in South Carolina on American-made paper and manufactured entirely in the United States. Products carrying the accredited Forest Stewardship Council (FSC) label are printed on 100 percent FSC-certified paper.

MADE IN THE USA